WALKING IN THE
BRIANÇONNAIS

About the Author

Andrew McCluggage was born in Northern Ireland, where he lives with his wife and two children. A hill-walking and mountain biking fanatic, he spends a large part of his time in the Briançonnais. After two decades as a corporate lawyer, he decided to do something more interesting and wrote this book.

WALKING IN THE BRIANÇONNAIS

40 WALKING ROUTES IN THE FRENCH ALPS EXPLORING HIGH MOUNTAIN LANDSCAPES NEAR BRIANÇON

by Andrew McCluggage

JUNIPER HOUSE, MURLEY MOSS,
OXENHOLME ROAD, KENDAL, CUMBRIA LA9 7RL
www.cicerone.co.uk

Printed by KHL Printing, Singapore
A catalogue record for this book is available from the British Library.
All photographs are by the author unless otherwise stated.

Route mapping by Lovell Johns www.lovelljohns.com
Contains OpenStreetMap.org data © OpenStreetMap
contributors, CC-BY-SA. NASA relief data courtesy of ESRI

The routes of the GR®, PR® and GRP® paths in this
guide have been reproduced with the permission of the
Fédération Française de la Randonnée Pédestre holder of
the exclusive rights of the routes. The names GR®, PR®
and GRP® are registered trademarks. © FFRP 2018 for all
GR®, PR® and GRP® paths appearing in this work.

Acknowledgements

Primarily thanks must go to my wife, Olive, with whom I have shared
hundreds of days in the mountains. If it was not for her support and hard
work looking after our children, this book would never have been written. Thanks also to the people in the Vallouise Valley who have warmly
welcomed us into their fold, and in particular to Pierrette Saint-Lebe,
our French guardian angel, for her generosity, friendship and advice. The
Bankes family also deserve a mention for their generosity and for intro-
ducing us to the Briançonnais in the first place. Finally thanks to our two
beautiful children, who put a smile on our faces even on the worst of days.

Front cover: A magical vista near les Arêtes de la Bruyère (Walk 37)

CONTENTS

Symbols used on route maps

		Relief
~	route	in metres
-,-	alternative route	5000 and above
(SF)	start/finish point	4800–5000
	glacier	4600–4800
	woodland	4400–4600
	urban areas	4200–4400
	regional border	4000–4200
	international border	3800–4000
—■—	station/railway	3600–3800
▲	peak	3400–3600
⬆	refuge	3200–3400
■	building	3000–3200
♁♁	church/chapel	2800–3000
Ⱳ	fort	2600–2800
)(	col	2400–2600
⌣⌢	bridge	2200–2400
⟟	chairlift	2000–2200
		1800–2000
		1600–1800
		1400–1600
		1200–1400
		1000–1200
		800–1000
		600–800
		400–600
		200–400
		0–200

SCALE: 1:50,000

0 kilometres 0.5   1

0 miles   0.5

Contour lines are
drawn at 25m intervals
and highlighted at
100m intervals.

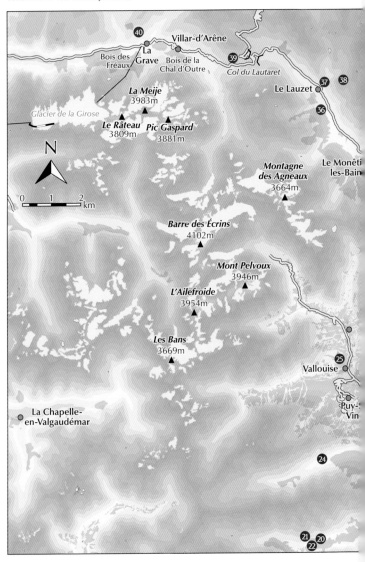

Wild flowers at l'Alpe du Lauzet (Walk 38)

Mountain safety

Every mountain walk has its dangers, and those described in this guidebook are no exception. All who walk or climb in the mountains should recognise this and take responsibility for themselves and their companions along the way. The author and publisher have made every effort to ensure that the information contained in this guide was correct when it went to press, but, except for any liability that cannot be excluded by law, they cannot accept responsibility for any loss, injury or inconvenience sustained by any person using this book.

International Distress Signal *(emergency only)*
Six blasts on a whistle (and flashes with a torch after dark) spaced evenly for one minute, followed by a minute's pause. Repeat until an answer is received. The response is three signals per minute followed by a minute's pause.

Helicopter Rescue
The following signals are used to communicate with a helicopter:

Help needed:
raise both arms
above head to
form a 'Y'

Help not needed:
raise one arm
above head, extend
other arm downward

Emergency telephone numbers
France: PGHM (Peloton de Gendarmerie de Haute Montagne):
Tel 04 50 53 16 89; Emergency services: Tel 112 (mobile phones)

Weather reports
France: Chamonix: Tel 08 92 68 02 74, www.meteo.fr or Tel 3250

Note Mountain rescue can be very expensive – be adequately insured.

View from the descent from Col des Marsailles (Walk 15)

INTRODUCTION

The glaciers of la Meije reflected in Lac Noir (Walk 40)

Dominated on all sides by jagged peaks, and perched on a rocky spur at the nucleus of five beautiful valleys, the city of Briançon lies almost at the southernmost tip of the main Alpine range. It is the highest city in France (at 1326m above sea level) and it is the beating heart of the Briançonnais, the region to which it gives its name.

The Briançonnais is a stunning mountain wilderness packed with everything one would expect from a high alpine environment: snow-capped peaks, green valleys and pastures filled with the sound of cow bells, sparkling alpine lakes full of trout, an abundance of wild flowers and a labyrinth of paths.

However, despite these attractions, the Briançonnais does not receive the volume of visitors that the wealthier, glitzier Northern Alps enjoy. It is geographically more isolated, being further from motorways and transport hubs such as Geneva. And often the area is overlooked in favour of mountains within national parks, which are more marketable. Yet anyone who has visited this amazing region will tell you that this is ludicrous. Although only part of the Briançonnais falls within a national park – the Écrins National Park (Parc National des Écrins) – it is as scenic and unspoilt as any mountain region in Europe.

In particular, the Briançonnais has largely been overlooked by English speaking walkers who have tended to favour the more easily accessible mountains around Geneva. This is a significant advantage for the walker who will find (save during the six peak summer weeks) largely empty tracks and paths among indescribable beauty. Outside of peak times it is not unusual to spend a whole day hiking in these wonderful mountains without encountering another soul. Even during peak times, the mountains here are tranquil compared to many other better known regions. In the age of mass tourism this is truly a rarity in the Alps. In short, those who favour solitude will feel like they have died and gone to heaven.

Such statements may sound like tourist office hyperbole, but they are supported by statistics. For example, the Écrins National Park (the northeast section of which contains part of the Briançonnais) is approximately half the size of the Lake District National Park in the UK, which attracts approximately 16 million visitors each year. Yet the Écrins National Park apparently only gets around 800,000 visitors. This suggests that the Briançonnais receives a mere 10 per cent of the visitors per km^2 that the Lake District attracts.

Perhaps as a consequence of the lack of visitors and its relative remoteness, the Briançonnais has not been exposed to as much development as the Northern Alps, retaining a rural feel which has largely died out elsewhere. The Hautes Alpes in which Briançon resides is one of the least affluent regions of France. It remains

Cervières and the Cerveyrette Valley as seen on the climb to l'Alp du Pied (Walk 12)

The beautiful Clarée Valley is a highlight of the region (Walk 8)

a French region for French people, and exhibits a charm often extinct in more touristy areas. Here, one finds few large ski resorts scarring the landscape. Absent, too, are the millionaires' chalets found elsewhere. This absence of development and pretension is one reason that aficionados of the region are fiercely loyal to it.

Another major draw is the climate. Briançon reputedly enjoys 300 days of sunshine each year, or so the locals are fond of saying. This may or may not be true in any particular year, but the climate is milder than the Northern Alps. For walkers this results in more sunny days, higher daytime and evening temperatures and less rain than in alpine regions further north. Anyone who has travelled hundreds of miles for a week's holiday in the mountains, only to be

forced indoors by inclement weather for most of that week, will readily confirm that favourable odds on sunshine are not to be discounted lightly.

To get a brief flavour of the region you could watch a stage of the Tour de France, the world's greatest cycling race, which takes place over three weeks each July. If the highlight of the race each year is its foray into the Alps, the highlight of each Alpine foray is often the race's journey into the Briançonnais. Make no mistake, this is one of cycling's true heartlands, soaked in almost a century of cycling history. Every few years the race passes through Briançon (sometimes twice!), or makes its tortuous way over one or more of the region's famous cycling cols, such as the Col du Galibier, the Col de Lautaret or the Col d'Izoard. Cycling fans will

The Torrent de l'Orceyrette just above the lake of the same name (Walk 19)

therefore have glimpsed the scale and majesty of these mountains. But walkers from outside France are unlikely to have even heard of the Briançonnais. And therein lies its charm!

As regards the geography of the region, five principal valleys (named after the rivers which flow along them) form the spokes of a cartwheel, with Briançon at the hub. Each valley has a section of this book devoted to it, and a detailed summary of each valley is set out below. Starting in the north, there is the picture postcard that is the Clarée Valley. Moving clockwise are the less visited mountains around the Cerveyrette Valley and the Ayes Valley, to the east. Then there is the part of the mighty Durance Valley, which runs just to the south of Briançon, together with three peaceful and little known tributaries which border the

Écrins National Park – the well hidden and unpopulated Fournel Valley, the tranquil Freissinières Valley and the Vallouise Valley, perhaps the jewel in the crown. The fifth spoke is the wide Guisane Valley to the west. Finally, the sixth section of this book focuses on the mountains to the northeast of the city around Montgenèvre, which are littered with hill forts and overlook the Italian border.

VALLEYS OF THE BRIANÇONNAIS AND MONTGENÈVRE

Clarée Valley

The Clarée Valley is, for many, the highlight of the Briançonnais, and is surely one of the most picturesque places in the Alps. A long, wide valley of stunning grassy pastures, it is bisected by the crystal clear, fast flowing River Clarée and flanked on both sides by wonderful snowy peaks. The villages in the valley are small and undeveloped and you get a clear sense of times gone by.

The opportunities for the walker here are myriad, and a book could be written on this magnificent alpine wilderness alone. Many of the routes in this valley are long but no apology is made: this is epic walking country.

Cerveyrette Valley

This idyllic valley is well known to road cyclists who use it to mount an assault on the famous Col d'Izoard. It is less frequented by walkers, however, which is surprising, given its appeal. The valley's main village is Cervières, which makes a lovely place to spend the night. There are also a number of charming hamlets, not least les Fonts, which has a refuge.

The valley stretches out to the southeast extremities of the Briançonnais, where it meets the stunning Queyras, another relatively unknown mountain range adjacent to the Italian frontier. If you are looking for peace and quiet then the Cerveyrette is the place. Take your time here and soak up the atmosphere among some very fine alpine scenery.

Ayes Valley

Owing to its relative inaccessibility, this small valley is one of the least frequented places in the Briançonnais.

The narrow access roads still have gravel surfaces in places. Although they are normally accessible to all vehicles, the going is slow. Use this as an excuse to take your time – those that make the effort will be rewarded with some of the most beautiful places that the region has to offer.

The walks described here are just a snapshot of those available, but they showcase many of its highlights – crystal clear lakes, historic forts, icy cols and snowy peaks. This valley should not be overlooked.

Durance Valley

The mighty River Durance runs more than 300km, all the way from its source near Montgenèvre to the River Rhône near Avignon. By the time it reaches Briançon it is already a wide and powerful torrent and is a dominant feature of the city and its surrounds. As it gushes south from Briançon through a wide valley with high mountains on both sides, it is nourished with water flowing through a series of unspoilt tributary valleys.

The walks in this section explore a number of these tributary valleys which are located on the fringes of the Écrins National Park. Each one has its own unique delights. There is the stunning Vallouise Valley, with its pretty villages and hamlets, which makes a fantastic base. There is the bucolic Freissinières Valley, with its sparkling high altitude lakes. And there is the little known Fournel Valley, with its staggering wild flower collection, including the famous and rare Chardon Bleu.

And this is only scratching the surface. There are so many valleys in this part of the region that it would take a lifetime to explore them all. Indeed an entire book could easily be devoted to this part of the Durance Valley alone. One thing is certain – if you take the time to walk one of the routes here then you will come back for more.

Guisane Valley

The wide and wonderful Guisane Valley, which runs southeast towards Briançon, has some of the best walking in the region, if not the whole of the Alps. The mountains on the north side of the valley separate the Guisane from the Clarée Valley and therefore any route there will offer amazing views down into the Clarée. Meanwhile, bordering the south side of the Guisane is the spectacular Écrins National Park so the walks in the Guisane normally offer magnificent views of that huge and very special mountain wilderness.

Needless to say, the walking in this part of the Briançonnais is exceptional. Once again, this is only a small selection of the available possibilities but it will be enough to whet your appetite for more.

Montgenèvre

Montgenèvre is a small but busy ski resort in the winter, yet it is relatively quiet in the summer. It sits on the Italian–French frontier and is the staging point for some incredible walking, with views extending west towards Briançon and the Écrins National Park, east into Italy and south over the Cerveyrette Valley and the Queyras.

As a ski resort, there is some ski infrastructure present, but it is small-scale and discrete and quickly recedes as you gain height after leaving the resort, so this should not put you off.

The walking here is varied. There are easy low level walks close to Montgenèvre, and strenuous high altitude outings such as the climb of Mont Chaberton. For those who are interested in hill fortifications, there is plenty to see here.

HISTORY

The Briançonnais formed part of the kingdom of the Celtic King Cottius, who accepted the protection of the Roman Emperor Augustus around 13BC. Cottius became the prefect of the region, and reported to Rome. Brigantium was the Roman name for Briançon. During the 5th century, with the weakening of the Roman Empire, the Briançonnais was incorporated into the Kingdom of Burgandy.

In AD534 the Kingdom of Burgandy was conquered by the Franks. With the decline of the Franks, the Briançonnais became part of the huge kingdom of Arles and Vienne which stretched all the way from Basle to the Mediterranean. Around

The well preserved stone buildings of the hamlet of Bouchier (Walk 27)

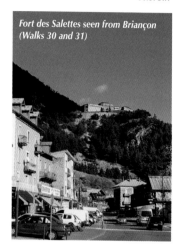

Fort des Salettes seen from Briançon (Walks 30 and 31)

1023 the Briançonnais came into the hands of the Counts of Albon, who became the Dauphins of Viennois, and in the 12th century it became part of the Dauphiné.

In the 13th and 14th centuries Briançon emerged as a prosperous market town benefitting from its prominent location on an important trading route between regions that are now part of France and Italy. The old town was constructed between 1196 and 1228. In 1343 the last Dauphin, Humbert II, conceded many of his feudal privileges to the Briançonnais, resulting in the formation of the République des Escartons du Briançonnais. The Dauphiné as a whole was sold to the French Crown in 1349.

The threat of a invasion of the Briançonnais by the House of Savoy led to substantial strengthening of Briançon's fortifications between 1692 and 1740. The architect of the work was the military engineer Marquis de Vauban (1633–1707), who shaped so many towns in France in the second half of the 17th century. He may not have overseen the construction of all of the fortifications (many of which were completed by later generations), but the idea of protecting the city with a ring of forts on the surrounding peaks and ridges was his. Briançon's Cité Vauban and other forts were part of these works (see Appendix B). Many of the forts are well preserved and a number of them are destinations of walks in this book.

In 1789 all traditional provinces in France were replaced by 83 *départements* answerable to the central government. This sounded the death

Fort de l'Olive with an autumn cloud inversion in the valley below (Walk 2)

knell for the République des Escartons du Briançonnais – the Briançonnais became part of the Département de l'Est Dauphine, which was later to become the Hautes Alpes, as it is known today. The French Revolution (1789–1799) led to occasional riots in the region, but the impact was minor when compared to many other areas of France.

Throughout the 19th century new military threats (including technological advancements with artillery) led to Vauban's fortifications being further strengthened. Some new forts were constructed during this period.

The Briançonnais saw no fighting during the First World War, but thousands of young men lost their lives fighting in other parts of France. During the Second World War, the region was occupied by the Italians (still allied with Germany) from 1940 to 1942: it is said that they were relatively civilised masters. When Italy switched sides in September 1943 things changed significantly, as a more stringent German presence was then maintained in Briançon. Various resistance organisations were active in the region, attacking German supply routes. Briançon was finally liberated in September 1944.

After the war, with the decline of traditional industries such as coal mining and silk production, the development of a ski resort at Chantemerle in the Guisane Valley, which had commenced in the 1930s, continued in earnest. In the 1950s and 1960s Serre Chevalier became firmly established as a credible ski resort. In the 1980s a ski lift was finally constructed in Briançon itself. Other than agriculture, tourism is the principal industry in Briançonnais.

WILDLIFE

There are many animals and birds which may be encountered in the Briançonnais. As a general rule of thumb, the earlier hours of the morning are best for sightings. Very often the first party on the trail may see many Chamois or Bouquetin, but following groups will not see any. The following is a list of key species to look out for:

Bouquetin (or **Ibex**) is a stocky goat-like animal, with long scimitar shaped horns. Hunted almost to extinction, it was saved by the Savoy kings who banned most hunting in 1821 and created a royal reserve in 1856 (which finally became Italy's Gran Paradiso National Park). Nowadays they are fairly widespread throughout the French Alps.

Chamois is another type of mountain goat which is smaller and slimmer than the Bouquetin, and has shorter horns which do not have deep ridges.

Deer are commonly seen, especially the Chevreuil (Roe Deer) which can be reddish or grey-brown, and the Daim (Fallow Deer) which tends to be brown with white spots. Deer are most likely to be spotted below the tree line.

Marmots are cute, fat, loveable rodents which are easy to spot. They live in colonies in grassy parts of the mountains and often you will see

A marmot never fails to put a smile on your face

them standing on their hind legs in the manner of a meerkat. Normally you will hear their sharp warning whistle before you see them.

Sanglier or **wild boar** are common in forests but are hard to spot. They can be best described as hairy brown pigs with tusks. If you are lucky enough to see one then keep your distance because they can be dangerous.

Wolves were hunted to extinction in France in the 1930s, but in recent years they have crossed into France from Italy (where conservation efforts have increased their numbers). The walker is highly unlikely to see one, but they are present in the Briançonnais.

Other mammals such as squirrels, foxes, badgers and mice are fairly common below the tree line.

Fish are found in most rivers, streams and lakes. Species of **trout** are common, and many high alpine lakes also contain **Arctic Char**.

A Bouquetin relaxing near l'Aiguillette du Lauzet (Walk 38)

Lagopède (or **Ptarmigan**) is a grouse-like bird. Its plumage is white in the winter and largely brown in the summer.

Gypaète Barbu (or **Bearded Vulture**) is a vulture with a wing-span of up to 3m. Its German name is 'Lammergeier', which means 'lamb-hawk', stemming from the belief that the bird attacked lambs. It occurs nat-urally at relatively low densities, so a sighting is something to be savoured. The good news is that a sighting in the Hautes Alpes is much more likely than further north. **Golden Eagles** can also be spotted in the region.

PASTOUS

The Briançonnais is still a very rural area, and many of the 'old ways' are still alive. Sheep are still walked up into the high mountains to graze at the end of spring each year, and brought back down again to winter in the low valleys. Even today, the shepherd will often live in a tiny cabin or mountain hut throughout the grazing season.

Traditionally, the flock would have had a dog (a 'Pastou' or 'Patou') to accompany it and to protect against bears, wolves and lynx. Wolves are once more a threat, so flocks of sheep in the Briançonnais still tend to have a Pastou attached to them. The Pastou is a very large, white, long haired dog which is related to an old Pyrenean breed. It will usually have been raised with the flock from a young age, so it forms a close bond with the sheep.

As they are working dogs whose job is to protect, they will often growl or bark if you approach the flock. Although uncommon, it is not unheard of for visitors to the French Alps to be bitten by a Pastou which felt that its sheep were being threat-ened. Accordingly, the best advice is

The view north from the amazing Lac de Cristol (Walk 32)

A flock of sheep in front of the Arêtes de la Bruyère (Walks 37 and 38)

to give them a wide berth. If you see a flock then it is wise to assume that there may be a Pastou with them. And be aware that from a distance the colour and texture of their coats makes them hard to spot amongst the sheep.

Notwithstanding the above advice, the author has had the following positive, although initially extremely unsettling, experience with a Pastou on the Col du Vallon in the Écrins National Park:

Early one beautiful morning in September, I sat alone on the top of the Col du Vallon enjoying the quality of light and solitude that can often only be found at that time of the morning. Lost in the splendour of the vista before me, the first thing I felt was light pressure on my back as something sat down behind me, so close that we were touching. Wondering who would have the audacity to invade my personal space in such a manner, I turned round and was shocked to come face to face with a goliath of a dog – a huge, shaggy, white Pastou. We were both seated, back to back, and yet its head towered above mine (or at least so it seemed!). My terror dissipated quickly, however, as he was gazing at me with the warm adoring eyes of a Labrador puppy. He gave me a lick on the cheek and when he lay down beside me, my instinctive reaction was to put my arm around him. We enjoyed ten minutes of the silent companionship that can only be experienced between a man/

woman and his/her dog. He then got up and simply wandered away back to his flock, without looking back.

Although heart warming, such experiences are likely to be few and far between, and under no circumstances should you use this anecdote as rationale for trying to pet a Pastou. To ensure that your day in the mountains does not take an unpleasant turn, view the Pastous from afar.

PLANTS AND FLOWERS

The Haute Alpes is a veritable cornucopia of wild flowers. At the right time of year you will be astounded by the myriad of colours and sheer variety of the flora on display. May and June are normally the best months for flowers, which wait patiently throughout the winter for the snow to clear and then rapidly spring to life. That said, there are still plenty of flowers in other months.

A few of the best known alpine flowers in the Briançonnais include the following:

Clockwise from left: Alpenrose, gentian, edelweiss and violas

Alpenrose is a bright pink member of the Rhododendron family and is seemingly everywhere at altitude in late June and July. They are particularly abundant on Walks 32 (Tour du Grand Area) and 20 (Lac Palluel and Lac Faravel).

Viola is a small flower which prefers grassy pastures. There are a variety of colours including yellow, white and blue (or a combination of those colours). Look out for them on Walk 3 near the Col des Thures.

Chardon Bleu is a rare blue flower which flowers between July and September. They are common at the top of the Fournel Valley near the start of Walk 24 (la Grande Cabane).

Edelweiss is probably the most famous alpine plant of all. This striking white flower is rare and only grows at high altitude (1800–3300m). It can be found (if you are lucky) on Walks 27 (Croix de la Salcette) and 40 (Plateau d'Emparis).

GETTING THERE

By air

The Briançonnais is well served by the following international airports and airlines:

- Turin (1hr 30min drive to Briançon) – Alitalia, British Airways, Easyjet, Ryanair
- Lyon (2hr 45min to Briançon) – Aer Lingus, British Airways, Easyjet
- Marseilles (2hr 50min to Briançon) – Aer Lingus, Air France, British Airways. Easyjet, Ryanair
- Milan Malpensa (3hr to Briançon) – Aer Lingus, Alitalia, British Airways, Easyjet
- Nice (3hr 30min to 5hr to Briançon depending upon the route) – Aer Lingus, Air France, British Airways, Easyjet, Ryanair.

This is not a complete list of airlines serving these airports but it will provide an idea of what is available.

Resalp runs bus services to Briançon from Lyon airport via Grenoble (see Appendix C). You can also get the train to Briançon from Marseille airport and Nice but you will need to change at least once (see http://en.oui.sncf). However, as you will need a car to access many of the walks, you might prefer to rent a car at the airport you fly into. All the major rental companies operate at the airports and cheap rates can be obtained via a booking website such as or www.holidayautos.co.uk. If you are flying into Italy (Turin or Milan) and propose to rent a car, check that your hire car company allows you to cross into France.

By train

Briançon is easily accessed from Paris by train. At the time of writing there is a daily overnight train in both directions between Briançon and Gare Austerlitz in Paris, but funding cuts may put this service under threat. It is an excellent service which offers reasonably priced sleeper carriages and gets into Briançon early in the morning. There are also a number of trains which run during the day to and from Gare de Lyon in Paris. Any of these train services could be linked with the Eurostar from London or a flight to Paris. Information on train times and tickets can be found at http://en.oui.sncf.

By car

You can bring your car to France from Ireland or the UK by one of the many ferry services (www.dfdsseaways.co.uk; www.stenaline.co.uk; www.irishferries.com; www.brittany-ferries.co.uk). Alternatively, you can travel with your car on the train from the UK through the channel tunnel (www.eurotunnel.com). The drive to the Briançonnais should take 9–10hr from arrival in France. If travelling from Calais or Dunkirk, take the road to Reims to avoid the busy ring road around Paris.

GETTING AROUND

Depending upon where you base yourself, you should be able to access some of the walks in this book by foot. In addition, many of the walks can be reached using local bus services. For example, regular buses travel to Montgenèvre and up and down the Guisane Valley between Briançon and la Grave. There are also daily Lignes Express Régionales buses travelling along the Durance Valley to and from Briançon (see Appendix C).

However, there are some walks in this book which will require you to have your own transport and, if you do, then you will get more out of the region. You could rent a car in Briançon but it is usually cheaper and easier to rent one on arrival at the airport (see 'Getting there').

WEATHER

Alpine climates tend to be drier and more predictable than those in mountain areas with a maritime climate (such as the UK or the US west coast). Nevertheless, as with any high mountain region, conditions can still change rapidly. It is prudent therefore to be prepared for rain and it is not beyond the realms of possibility to experience snow on high mountain passes ('cols') and summits even in the middle of summer. All mountains can be dangerous places and need to be treated with respect and caution, even if the weather forecast is favourable.

The weather in the Briançonnais can be extremely localised, often differing from valley to valley. It is possible therefore to climb to the top of a col in blazing sunshine only to find cloud or even rain over the other side. The Durance Valley has a slightly different climate, for example, than the Guisane.

Forecasts in France are relatively easy to access. National and regional forecasts can be found on television or radio. Local forecasts can be found

The Vallouise Valley in winter

at tourist information offices and most mountain huts will display up-to-date weather forecasts. Indeed, often the most reliable forecast can be that provided by a hut *gardien* (manager), as it will be infused with a wealth of local knowledge.

In addition, there are numerous internet sites, both French and international, which produce forecasts of varying reliability. One of the best sites is Meteo France, the French meteorological office, which provides regularly updated national, regional and local forecasts at www. meteofrance.com. Meteo France also has an excellent smart phone app which provides detailed local forecasts.

WHEN TO GO

In general the Briançonnais can be walked from May to October but, as with any part of the Alps, walking at altitude is restricted for part of the year by snow. Normally high cols will be snow covered until mid to late June, with the main walking season running from the end of June to the end of September. This does not mean that you cannot walk at other times and, indeed, it can be preferable to do so.

Spring (May and June): there is still plenty of excellent walking below the snowline to please the most hardened walker. Take care when approaching the snowline in spring, as avalanches are not uncommon and can kill. Away from the snowline

Wild flowers in spring in the Fournel Valley

you should have few concerns, and this can be the most beautiful time of year for walking: new growth will be on the trees, the weather is often sunny and warm and the peaks are frequently at their most photogenic, still frosted with snow. Visibility is generally excellent in the absence of summer haze. Of course there is still rain at this time of year, but this usually lessens as spring develops.

Furthermore, in May and early June the Briançonnais' hundreds of varieties of wild flowers are at their glorious best, the pastures resplendent with colour. This is a sight which most walkers, focused on the summer season, never get to see, and it cannot be recommended highly enough.

Additionally, the Briançonnais is extremely quiet during this period, so if you are seeking solitude then this is a great time to visit.

Summer (July and August): normally most of the high cols are passable on foot. This is the peak season, reaching its crescendo in the four weeks commencing around 14th July, when most of the French take their annual vacations. During these four weeks visitor numbers are at the summer maximum, yet when compared to the more popular Northern Alps it does not really seem busy at all.

Temperatures will be at their peak, reaching more than 30°C. Mornings are often clear and sunny, heating up as the sun rises into deep blue skies.

If there is to be cloud, this will likely form throughout the afternoon, and may bring thunderstorms. Sensible advice is to start early in the morning and get your main climb done while the temperature is cooler. Summer can be hazier than spring or autumn.

Autumn (September and October): visitor numbers thin out rapidly from the last week in August. French and Italian holiday-makers are back at work and the mountains are almost deserted (particularly mid-week). From the middle of September the mountain huts and gîtes start to close up for the season.

Often September offers the best walking, with settled weather and more comfortable temperatures than in summer. The skies are clear and visibility is normally excellent, particularly if your visit coincides with

the Mistral, a strong, cold northwest wind. Evenings will be cooler.

Walkers generally ignore October, which is a shame as the weather can be beautiful, and the proliferation of larch trees and other deciduous plants means that the autumn colours are an astounding mix of yellows, reds and browns. Days will be shorter so start walking early in October – if something were to go wrong you would have much less daylight to seek help than in the summer, which should also be borne in mind when deciding what to bring with you.

WHERE TO BASE YOURSELF

The main town in the Briançonnais is Briançon, which is also the most central place to stay. Details of tourist information can be found in Appendix

The Guisane Valley in autumn

29

The magnificent setting of the village of Vallouise

C. Briançon is well served by accommodation and restaurants and the historical old town is fascinating, but after a night or two most walkers will prefer to locate themselves somewhere more rural. The fantastic towns, villages and hamlets in the region are too numerous to list exhaustively but the following all make good bases.

Vallouise (www.tourisme-lavallouise.com tel +33 (0)4 92 23 36 12) is set in the stunning Vallouise Valley about 20min from Briançon and is perhaps the nicest place to stay. In the centre, there is a lovely 15th century church, a supermarket, a hotel and a couple of shops and restaurants. There are also hotels, gîtes and campsites nearby. In the peak summer season bookings should be made in advance. There is great mountain biking and via ferrata here too, and equipment can be rented in the valley.

Névache (www.nevache-tourisme. fr tel +33 (0)4 92 20 02 20). Located towards the top of the Clarée Valley, 20min drive from Briançon, its bucolic setting makes for a relaxing place to stay. There are some hotels, gites and restaurants and a beautiful campsite beside the river.

Montgenèvre (www. montgenevre.com tel +33 (0)4 92 21 52 52), a popular ski resort about 15min from Briançon, has many hotels and restaurants.

Le Monetier-les-Bains (www. serrechevalier.com/www.serre-chevalier.com tel +33 (0)4 92 24 98 98) is an attractive little town between Briançon and la Grave. It is home to a fantastic natural spring complex and plenty of restaurants and places to stay.

La Grave (www.lagrave-lameije. com tel +33 (0)4 76 79 90 05) is a pretty town set in front of the famous mountain la Meije (3983m). The many hotels, restaurants and bars are perfectly situated for those who wish to soak up the view of this permanently snowy peak. For something different to do, there is a cable car from the town up to the Glacier de la Girose.

ACCOMMODATION

Accommodation of all types is plentiful throughout the Briançonnais. During the French summer holidays it's advisable to book ahead. Outside of these times you should have no problems finding a pleasant place to stay, but be aware that in early spring and from mid-September onwards some accommodation will be closed.

Hotels

The range of available hotel accommodation is wide but quality can vary. The majority of hotels will be in the one to three star categories. There are a few four star hotels, but the five star is a very rare species indeed. Most hotels will offer breakfast and evening meals and the half board rates can be very good. These days many hotels are part of the Logis chain and details of their hotels can be found at www.logishotels.com. In this digital age, independent hotels in the region normally have their own websites too.

Self-catering chalets and apartments

For those wishing to stay in the same place for a week or more, self catering accommodation can be excellent value, particularly for families or groups. It is not too difficult to find a high quality chalet or apartment with a garden or terrace and a very fine view. Most *immobiliers* (estate agents) rent self-catering accommodation. However, English speakers may find it easier to avail of the good rates that can be found with Alp Base (see Appendix C).

Gîtes d'étape

A *gîte* is a difficult thing to define. Traditionally it would have been akin to a youth hostel, offering beds in dormitories and evening meals. Nowadays, however, as travellers are more demanding, gîtes are more upmarket – private rooms are normally available and blankets have largely been replaced by duvets. The accommodation in some gîtes is in fact better than many hotels but it pays to check before you book. Many gîtes now have their own websites.

Chambres d'hôte

Generally these approximate to bed and breakfast accommodation in the UK. Quality can vary widely – some can be better than hotels but others are little more luxurious than a mountain hut.

Refuges

These are mountain huts which offer dormitory accommodation and meals. Many also have private rooms. Duvets and sheets are becoming the norm and hopefully the itchy blanket is a thing of the past. To stay in a refuge, you will need to bring a sleeping sheet, a thin bag made of silk or cotton. These can be purchased cheaply at most outdoor shops in the UK or France or, sometimes, they can be rented for a small charge.

Refuges are often located deep within the mountains and accessible only to the walker. This is mountain travel at its finest, with no need to carry heavy gear or food. Wine and beer is usually available and if you are lucky the gardien may let you try his secret stash of homemade Génépy, a potent liqueur made from a plant only found in the high mountains. Most importantly refuges are good value – a bed for the night, dinner and breakfast should cost less than €50.

Campsites

Most towns and villages will have campsites and the services which they offer vary greatly. They will all have toilet and shower facilities but some have swimming pools and restaurants too. Wild camping or bivouacking may be tolerated provided that you only stay for a night. If you do camp out ensure that you carry out all rubbish and bury any toilet waste well away from watercourses.

Briançon viewed from the well preserved city walls (Walk 30)

SAFETY

On a sunny day the Alps can appear to be a benign paradise, but it only takes a change in the weather or a twisted ankle to turn a pleasant day out into something potentially life threatening. This should not put you off, but it is wise to treat the mountains with the respect they deserve and to be aware of your own experience levels and physical capabilities. The following is a non-exhaustive list of recommendations.

- Read walk descriptions carefully and make plans based on the abilities of the weakest member of your party.
- Get an up-to-date weather forecast (see 'Weather' above) and carefully reconsider your plans in light of the forecast. Never set out on long or exposed routes if the weather is uncertain.
- Get as fit as possible before you begin your vacation; the fitter you are the more you will enjoy walking.
- Start early to avoid having to ascend during the hottest part of the day and to give you more time in case something goes wrong.
- Buy a map. The maps in this book are indicative only and are no substitute for a sheet map.
- Before setting out, tell someone where you are going and what time you will return.
- Carry surplus food and clothing in case you have an accident or get held up by the weather.

- Never be afraid to turn back if you find the going too tough or if the weather deteriorates. It is better to fail on one occasion in order to succeed a hundred times in the future.
- Do not stray from the path (unless the route does not have one) to avoid getting lost. This will also avoid erosion of the landscape.
- Avoid exposed high ground in a thunderstorm. If you get caught out in one then drop your walking poles and stay away from trees, overhanging rocks, metal structures and caves. The generally accepted advice is to squat on your pack and keep as low as possible.
- In the event of an accident, move the injured person into a safe place and administer any necessary first aid. Keep the victim warm. Establish your exact coordinates and, if possible, use your mobile to call for help. The emergency number is 112. If you have no signal then send someone for help.
- Mountain biking is becoming more and more popular so keep your wits about you to avoid a collision.
- Hunting is popular in the Briançonnais. The season starts at the beginning of September and lasts throughout the autumn and early winter. It is sensible to wear something brightly coloured when walking in the hunting season.

FOOD AND DRINK

French food is generally excellent. Most hotels, gîtes and refuges will offer breakfast and evening meals. Breakfast will normally be coffee, bread and jam, perhaps with some cheeses or cold meats. Evening meals are usually substantial three course affairs as walkers tend to be hungry people. Soup and pâté are common starters and the main course will normally be some sort of meat with vegetables, rice, pasta or salad. This will often be followed by dessert or cheese.

Many of the restaurants will serve local specialities such as *Tourtons*, otherwise improbably known as *Coussins du petit Jésus* (Cushions of baby Jesus). These are tasty little pastry squares stuffed with fillings such

GENERAL INFORMATION

Language: French is the first language but many locals will have at least some basic English.

Money: France uses the euro (€). ATMs can be found in most towns but rarely in smaller villages. Credit cards are accepted widely although most refuges accept cash only.

Visas: citizens of the European Union do not need a visa. At the time of writing citizens of Australia, New Zealand, Canada and the US do not need a visa for stays of up to three months. Brexit may change things for the UK traveller.

Mobile phones: mobiles should work in towns and villages. In the mountains, however, it can be hit and miss. 3G services are widely available so access to the internet from smart phones is often possible.

International dialling codes: the country code for France is +33 and the first 0 in the French area code is omitted if calling from outside of France.

Internet: many hotels and gîtes now have wifi but refuges do not.

Insurance: mountain rescue services may not be free and therefore it is wise to ensure that you have adequate insurance which covers hiking. Visitors from the UK should also make sure that they have the free European Health Insurance Card (EHIC) but remember that in France this will only cover part of your medical treatment so insurance is still recommended. Also, the EHIC will not cover mountain rescues. With Brexit looming it is possible that the EHIC card may soon be a thing of the past for UK residents and in such circumstances private insurance will become even more important.

Emergencies: the emergency telephone number is 112.

The pretty chapel in Névache

as potato, cheese or meat. Fondues and *tartiflette* (a rich and tasty concoction of potatoes, cream, ham and Reblochon cheese) are also popular mountain fares.

Bread is nothing short of a way of life in France and is consistently excellent – most towns and villages will have a *boulangerie* (bakery). Supermarkets in France stock a wide range of fantastic cheeses and cold meats so picnic food is readily available.

Many towns and villages have popular weekly markets at which there will be stalls selling bread, cheeses, meats and other locally made products. These markets are well supported by locals and visitors alike and tourist information offices can provide information on them. Perhaps one of the most enjoyable is the Thursday morning market in

Vallouise, where the stalls are set up in the old village centre.

VIA FERRATA

A few of the routes in the book can be varied to link them with via ferrata routes. *Via ferrata* is an Italian phrase which literally means 'iron road'. It is commonly associated with the First World War, when steel ladders were bolted into rock faces in the Italian Dolomites to assist with the movement of Italian troops. In recent years, modern via ferratas have been constructed in the French Alps. Crête de la Rortie (Walk 23) could be combined with an excellent via ferrata and L'Aiguillette du Lauzet (Walk 38) also has a via ferrata.

A via ferrata enables people with no rock climbing experience to ascend a rock face with the assistance of ladders, steps and cables (onto which the user should be clipped at all times). You should always be properly equipped with a twin lanyard and carabiner set, helmet, gloves and harness. Get instruction from an experienced professional unless you know what you are doing. Tackling a via ferrata is an exhilarating experience which can be the highlight of many people's trip to the mountains, but it should not be treated lightly and should not be attempted by anyone who does not have a good head for heights. A fall during a via ferrata climb could lead to serious injury or even death.

Full information on how to do a via ferrata is beyond the scope of this book. They are mentioned here in passing to make the reader aware of possible alternatives on particular walks but the book does not provide detailed route descriptions for the specific via ferrata routes or information on how to do a via ferrata safely. A good reference point is Richard Miller's excellent book *Via Ferratas of the French Alps* (Cicerone Press, 2014).

WHAT TO TAKE

Having the wrong equipment or clothing can make a day out in the mountains uncomfortable, unpleasant or even dangerous. You should be adequately equipped for the terrain and for the worst weather conditions which you could possibly face. Being cold and wet at high altitude is no fun and can put you at risk.

Weight is also worth taking into account – if you take too little then you might not be properly prepared, but if you take too much then that 1000m ascent will be more difficult.

Boots should be good quality, properly fitting and worn in. Good ankle support and thick cleated soles (such as Vibram) are recommended.

Good quality **walking socks** are as important as boots and they should fit properly and be quick drying.

A good quality **waterproof jacket** is vital even if the forecast looks dry. Breathable fabrics are the norm. It is also wise to carry **waterproof trousers** although you may rarely need them.

Layering is important. On your upper body wear a **base layer** (which will wick moisture outwards from your body) with a **fleece** on top as a mid-layer. For added warmth you can put on your waterproof. Depending on the season, you may wish to bring additional layers. On your legs wear **shorts** or **trousers**, depending on the season. Always carry a warm **hat** and **gloves** just in case. Bear in mind that in October if you start early in the morning the temperature could be -5°C but by noon it can reach 18–19°C.

Your **rucksack** should have well padded shoulder straps and waist band. Much of the weight of the pack should sit on your hips rather than your shoulders. A waterproof liner to go into your pack can be a good investment.

Poles will transfer some of the weight from your legs onto your arms keeping your legs a little fresher. On descents they can save your knees and can reduce the likelihood of falling or twisting an ankle.

Carry a basic **first aid kit** at all times. A small **torch** with **spare batteries** and a **whistle** are sensible additions – many rucksacks have whistles incorporated into the sternum strap. A **space blanket** or **emergency bag** is very light and could save someone's life.

Always carry a **map and compass** and know how to use them. A **GPS** can be a useful addition but it is

Hiking with a baby towards Col des Cibière (Walk 34)

no substitute for a map and compass – after all, batteries can run out and electronics can fail.

The sun at altitude can be brutal so wear **sunscreen** and **lip salve**. **Sunglasses** and a **sun hat** are also recommended

Carry at least 1.5 litres of **water** per person

MAPS

IGN is the French public geographical service, producing a range of maps covering French territory in various scales and formats. Each walk description in this book contains information on the appropriate 1:25,000 scale map(s).

USING THIS GUIDE

The walks in this book are only a taste of the hundreds of possibilities available in this amazing region. Six geographical areas are covered and you could easily spend a week or more in each area. Routes could be shortened or lengthened to meet your needs. A route summary table is provided in Appendix A as a useful aid for choosing a walk.

Walk grading: walks have been graded easy, medium, hard or very hard. Walk grading is subjective: one person's hill is another person's mountain. The grades in this book take account of distance, ascent, gradient, terrain and navigational challenge. If there is difficult terrain or significant exposure on a walk then this can impact its categorisation. In general, a walk graded easy could be undertaken by most people. A walk graded very hard is only suitable for fit and experienced walkers.

Timings: these indicate the time for a reasonably fit walker to complete the walk. They do not include any resting time.

Distances: distance is measured in kilometres, to match maps and signposts in France. One mile equates to 1.6km.

Total ascent and descent: the total ascent is the aggregate of all the altitude gain on the uphill sections of the walk. Total descent is the aggregate of the height losses on the downhill sections. Ascent and descent are measured in metres. As a rule of thumb, a fit walker climbs 300–400m in an hour.

Maps: each walk contains a sketch map: these are indicative only and are no substitute for the detail on the full 1:25,000 scale sheet maps. The correct map for each walk is highlighted in the walk description. You are less likely to get lost or take a wrong turning if you use the recommended maps (see 'Maps').

Signposting: yellow signposts giving time or distance to a specific destination are common and tend to be quite reliable. Painted red and white stripes on rocks and trees are sometimes used as waymarks. If you see a cross painted on a rock or a tree then this generally means that you are going in the wrong direction. Plastic 'VTT' signs nailed to trees are for mountain biking routes – take care as mountain bikes move quickly and any collision between walkers and a mountain bike is likely to have serious consequences. The VTT (Vélo Tout Terrain) route may or may not be along the same route as you need to follow so don't rely these signs as your own waymarks.

GPS coordinates: each walk description includes coordinates for the starting point. Occasionally, within the route description, coordinates are also provided for junctions which are tricky to locate. These coordinates are given in the UTM-WGS84 format used by the IGN maps. For Suunto watches set your position format to 'UTM'.

Signposts at Col de l'Oule (Walk 34)

CLARÉE VALLEY

Larch trees resplendent with autumn colours in the Clarée Valley (Walk 2)

WALK 1
Col de Dormillouse

Start/finish	La Draye near Val-des-Prés (1400m, UTM 32T 316871 4980684)
Distance	14km
Ascent/descent	1100m
Grade	Hard
Time	5hr 30min
Maximum altitude	2445m
Map	IGN 3536OT Briançon (1:25,000)
Refreshments	None
Access	From Briançon take the N94 towards Montgenèvre. After a few kms take the D994 left (N) up the Clarée Valley towards Névache. N of Val-des-Prés, after the bridge at the hamlet of la Draye, there is a large car park on the left.

A beautiful foray into the high alpine pastures of the Clarée Valley, where sheep have grazed for centuries. The walk climbs through pristine forest to a classic hanging valley before reaching the lovely Col de Dormillouse, where the views are spectacular. Route finding can be tricky for the first hour as there are a number of interconnecting paths. At the time of writing, recent landslides in the Ravin de la Lauze have buried some small sections of path and a little scrambling over rocks was required to locate the path again. Helpfully, a few cairns had been placed to assist with navigation in these areas. Care should be taken approaching the Ravin des Fournéous as the path is a little unstable in places.

The descent passes historical alpine farmers' huts and cabins. These huts provide a fascinating insight into the conditions endured by the shepherds of times gone by, whose pastures were made famous by Emilie Carles' autobiography, *A Wild Herb Soup* (1977), describing the plight of local farming communities in the 19th and early 20th centuries (see box below).

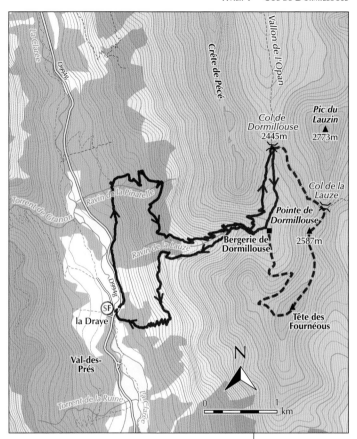

From the NE side of the car park, follow the signposts to 'Grotte de Cinquante Anes' and 'Dormillouse'. Cross the road and follow a track on the other side, heading E towards a yellow signpost. At the signpost turn left ('Grotte de Cinquante Anes') and follow a small path to the N which runs parallel to the road. After 10min, the path meets a faint track – turn right. There are some yellow waymarks to guide you.

Eventually, the path starts to head away from the road – continue N to arrive at the **Ravin de la Pinatelle** (35min). Cross the ravine in a NE direction and continue on a path on the other side. Shortly after the ravine, at a track, turn right, uphill (E). Where the track bears back around to the N, ignore a faint track on the right. Shortly afterwards, ignore a path on the left and continue to climb up the track.

When the track meets the ravine again (at what appears to be a dead end), turn left to follow a small path heading up to the left (N) – the start of the path is concealed behind some bushes and is a little tricky to locate. The path zigzags up the slope and just below a large needle shaped rock formation arrives at a junction of paths: turn right to continue uphill (SE). The path soon arrives back at the ravine and here the path splits – keep right to climb parallel to the ravine for a few moments. The path then crosses the ravine to pick up a path on the other side, heading S.

Shortly after crossing the ravine, the path bears around to the left – ignore a faint path here to the right heading S. ◄ After 5min, arrive at another junction of paths – keep straight ahead (S) still following yellow waymarks.

Eventually, the path arrives at a fork and two signs (2hr): turn left, following a sign for 'Dormillouse' up the N side of the **Ravin de la Lauze**. As you climb, the views into the Clarée Valley become better and better. Watch your footing as the rocky path is narrow and unstable in places.

Where the path meets the base of the ravine and disappears, head straight up the N edge of the ravine (following cairns) and after a minute find the path again on your left (heading W). After another 5min, ignore a path on the left by a cairn and keep straight ahead (E), following yellow waymarks.

Where the path meets a little ravine, cross over and scramble up the other side towards a cairn. ◄ From here on, the rocky path becomes hard to follow in places so concentration is essential.

Yellow waymarks will confirm that you are on the correct route.

At the time of writing, there had been a small landslide here making the path tricky to follow.

Where the path arrives at a junction of faint paths
(3hr), turn left, signposted 'Col de Dormillouse'. Red
waymarks guide you here. Soon the path leaves the grass
to climb initially W up a rocky slope. The path zigzags up
the face of the slope until finally, it passes below a rocky
outcrop and then proceeds N to **Col de Dormillouse**
(2445m, 3hr 30min). The magnificent views extend to the
N down the Vallon de l'Opon and to the E and S you can
gaze up to the jagged lines of the Crête de la Lauze. The
col is flanked to the W by the Crête de Pécé and to the E
by the Pic du Lauzin.

> You are on the **GR5** here and, should you be feeling
> particularly energetic, you could follow it to the SE
> up to the Col de la Lauze. From there you could fol-
> low the ridge to the S to the Tête des Fournéous and
> then descend down to the Bergerie de Dormillouse
> to rejoin the walk. This variant is stunning but
> would add approximately 3hr to the walk.

From the col, take a path heading SE. After a few
metres head S down a grassy spur towards the base of the

*The view N from the
Col de Dormillouse*

An old shepherd's cabin below the Col de Dormillouse

grassy valley below. Keep heading S along the base of the valley. When you catch a glimpse of a shepherds' cabin below to the S, make your way towards it. The path is intermittent but the grassy terrain is straightforward.

Arrive at the stone building of **la Bergerie de Dormillouse** (4hr). The views from the bergerie into the Clarée Valley are beautiful. ◄

Nearby are more recent huts. The difference between what shepherds use today and the old stone huts is stark.

Pass to the right of the bergerie and descend the grassy slope to the SW – watch where you place your feet as there are a lot of marmot burrows here.

Upon reaching the **Ravin de la Lauze** again, cross over and pick up a small path heading down the S side of the ravine. The path is faint at times but there are plenty of red and black waymarks. Eventually the path moves away from the middle of the ravine and heads into the forest.

When the path emerges from the trees onto a grassy plateau (4hr 30min), with fabulous views of the Clarée Valley, keep descending, passing to the left of an old stone ruin. Shortly after the ruin, the path bears around to the N and enters the trees again. After a few minutes, arrive at a junction of paths – turn left and descend on a small path.

Eventually, the path emerges from the trees and works its way along the base of some cliffs – the path here is narrow in places and there are steep drops, so be careful. Then the path zigzags S down the slope and enters the trees again. Finally, the path arrives at a track – turn right and immediately afterwards, turn left (W) to descend on a path. Where the path meets another faint track, turn right and continue downhill back to the car park (5hr 30min).

EMILIE CARLES

Emilie Carles, the most famous resident of the Clarée Valley, was born in 1900 into a peasant farming family. Her mother died when she was four and she managed to juggle strenuous farm work, helping to look after her family and trying to attend school to gain an education. The Clarée Valley in those days was remote and bitterly poor and opportunities for advancement for its children were few and far between. Against all odds, Emilie managed to qualify as a teacher and taught in a number of impoverished peasant farming communities throughout the Haute Alpes before returning to Val-des-Prés. She loved the Clarée Valley with all her heart and spent the rest of her life here.

In 1977 she published her memoirs, in the French language, to popular acclaim. *Une Soupe aux Herbes Sauvages* was published in English in 1991 as *A Wild Herb Soup – The life of a French Countrywoman*.

Describing in detail the terrible conditions and difficulties endured by the region's farming communities in the 19th and early 20th centuries, the book is shocking in its frankness and highlighted in particular the challenges for the women in these communities, upon whom much of the work appeared to fall (despite having to bear child after child in a era without effective birth control). The conditions they endured were shocking relative to living standards in modern day France.

The book did not always paint the residents of Val-des Prés in a good light. In particular, local officials were often painted as petty, chauvinistic and resistant to progress. This caused some resentment and, although Emilie Carles became famous and feted throughout France, it is said that some bitterness still remains among a few in the Clarée Valley.

In the 1970s there was talk of construction of a motorway to Turin in Italy which would traverse the Clarée Valley. Emilie, fearing that a motorway would destroy the valley's pristine environment, lobbied relentlessly against the project. She was instrumental in creating a protection association for the valley. There followed posters, pamphlets, petitions and hearings. Protests and marches were held in Briançon and elsewhere to highlight the Valley's plight. In October 1975 she held a press conference in Paris in which she explained how the motorway would affect small farmers and argued that France had an absolute duty to protect nature in the valley. Gradually the protest expanded and in 1976 the project was abandoned. Emilie died in 1979, and in 1992 the Clarée Valley was finally given protected status.

Little has changed here in generations. The valley remains a stunning rural environment of snowy peaks, green pastures and icy streams, and it depends for its survival on both tourism and agriculture. Without the single-mindedness of Emilie Carles, the beauty and tranquillity of this pristine environment may have been lost forever.

The descent offers magnificent views of the Clarée Valley

WALK 2

Fort de l'Olive and Fort de Lenlon

Start/finish	Plampinet (1482m, UTM 32T 315611 4985942)
Distance	17km
Ascent/descent	1050m
Grade	Hard
Time	6hr
Maximum altitude	2508m
Map	IGN 3535OT Névache (1:25,000) and IGN 3536OT Briançon (1:25,000)
Refreshments	Plampinet
Access	From the top of Briançon take the N94 towards Montgenèvre. After about 3km, exit at la Vachette and take the D994 all the way to Plampinet. Drive over the bridge in the village and immediately afterwards there is a parking area on the right.

For those interested in military history this walk is second to none, visiting two very different forts and with traces of history in evidence throughout. The views into the Clarée Valley are absolutely superb. The walk is long and the rocky tracks hard on your feet but on a fine day it's more than worth it. There is nothing too technical about the route save that the section just before the metal door below the Fort de l'Olive is very steep and has some loose rock.

From the car park, cross over the road and proceed N along a path running parallel to the road. Shortly afterwards, arrive at a small chapel and take a track to the NW, in the direction of a signpost to 'Névache'. After 15–20min, at a fork, take a track on the left following a sign to 'Fort de l'Olive'.

After another 10 minutes, arrive at a junction of tracks – pass between two cairns on the left onto a path, following the sign for 'Fort de l'Olive'. The rocky path

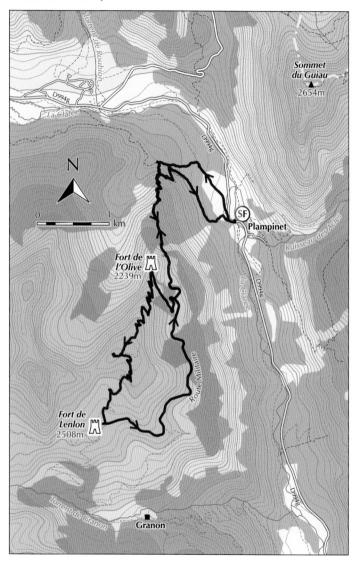

winds its way steeply upwards, generally towards the S. At a signpost turn right uphill. ▶ Where the path levels off, if you look up, you will get your first glimpse of Fort de l'Olive. Eventually, the path proceeds across a shale slope and from here you get fantastic views towards Plampinet.

After the shale slope, the path becomes very steep for a while and then arrives at a large metal door giving access below the fort (1hr 40min). Go through the door and keep straight ahead on a track for 10–15min to a signpost. Turn right along a track signposted 'Fort de l'Olive'. You can see the fort up ahead of you. The winding track may seem like a rather roundabout way of getting to the fort but it will be worth it. Forts are supposed to be impregnable, after all, so access is never going to be easy!

At the top is **Fort de l'Olive** (2239m, 2hr 30min), perched precipitously on the side of the mountain. It is well worth taking some time to explore.

The path going downhill to the left will be the route of the descent later on.

Larch trees in the Clarée valley showing their autumn colours

49

FORT DE L'OLIVE

As technology advanced and the range of artillery increased, it became necessary to construct a series of outlying forts around Briançon to protect against enemy batteries whose cannons could now reach the city. Fort de l'Olive was built between 1881 and 1883 to help counter threats from the Italian border and in particular to control the Col de l'Echelle and the Col des Thures.

The fort was relatively small, with 14 rooms which garrisoned about 200 soldiers, but the surrounding walls cover a large area of about 2.5 hectares. The batteries were situated on two levels at the NE corner. In 1934 two pillboxes housing 75mm guns were constructed to counter the threats posed from the battery on the summit of Mont Chaberton. Such was the importance of Fort de l'Olive that between 1891 and 1893, Fort de Lenlon was built to defend it from the rear.

Facing the front of the fort, turn left onto a path heading to a little stone hut that can be seen above to the SW. Pass the hut and keep climbing on the track. Soon Fort de Lenlon comes into view to the SW. Shortly afterwards, leave the track in favour of a path which can be seen running across the hillside to the SW – you can stay on the track all the way up to Fort de Lenlon if you wish but the path should make for a quicker approach. At times the path disappears but the terrain is relatively easy so just keep heading directly to the fort. Soon you will arrive at **Fort de Lenlon** (2508m, 3hr).

Descend from the fort using the track and follow it towards the E. After a few minutes, the track splits. Follow it around to the right – the left fork would take you back to Fort de l'Olive. The track twists and turns down across the hillside, generally towards the S (passing many interesting military barracks and other buildings along the way). The track's route is circuitous, so now and again you may wish to take shortcuts across some of the hairpins.

3hr 45min from the start, the path joins an old **military track** at a signpost (2302m). Turn left (E) following a sign to 'Fort de l'Olive' and 'Plampinet'. The track descends gently for about an hour and the views into the

A chilly morning at Fort de Lenlon

Clarée Valley are incredible. The only downside is that the rocks on the track make for slightly uncomfortable walking and the track seems to go on forever. ▶

4hr 45min from the start you'll reach the signpost you passed earlier (just before the final climb to Fort de l'Olive). Keep right, following the sign for 'Plampinet'. Pass through the metal door again and descend on the path of your ascent. The descent is initially quite tricky and steep. When you reach a signpost keep straight ahead towards 'Plampinet' (on a different path from that which you climbed up).

At a T-junction marked by a large cairn, turn right. Keep along this path for quite some time. Eventually, the path comes down out of the trees to pass through open pastures, with Plampinet just on the right. Before you come to the little chapel at the main road (which you passed at the start of the walk), take a little path to the right running behind a cemetery. Follow this all the way back to the car park (6hr).

Do not become disillusioned by the distances and times shown on the signs along the military track as they do not always appear to be correct.

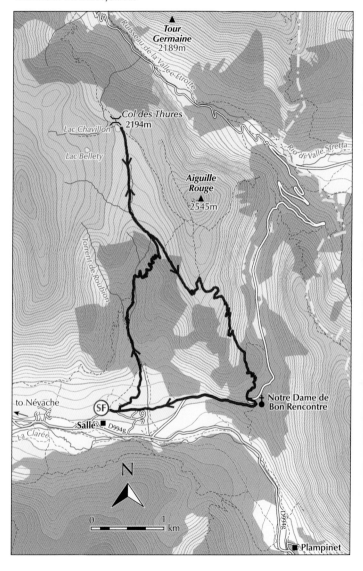

WALK 3
Col des Thures

Start/finish	Sallé near Névache (1610m, UTM 32T 313180 4987900)
Distance	14.25km
Ascent/descent	740m
Grade	Hard
Time	4hr 25min
Maximum altitude	2220m
Map	IGN 3535OT Névache (1:25,000)
Refreshments	Restaurants in Névache
Access	From the top of Briançon take the N94 towards Montgenèvre. After about 3km exit at la Vachette onto the D994 to Névache. On arriving at Névache, look carefully for a wooden sign on the right for 'Sallé' (it is easy to miss). Turn right onto Rue de Sallé and follow this narrow road to the 'Champ Bellet' car park on the left.

This walk is a Clarée classic. It involves a visit to the beautiful Col des Thures near the mighty Mont Thabor (3178m) and a very pretty lake, with lovely views back into the Clarée Valley and beyond. The final few kilometres of the route involve a magnificent stroll along the base of the Clarée Valley towards Névache.

Although the route is quite long, it poses few difficulties in terms of navigation or terrain. However, due to its popularity, in the summer months it is wise to set off early.

From the car park go back out onto the road and turn left (E). After about 150m is a small road on the left called 'Chemin des Ames'. Head up this road, which soon turns into a gravel track. After 15mins walking, a wooden board indicates 'Forêt Dominale de la Clarée': go through a barrier and keep straight ahead on the track. ▶

After another 10min, cross a wooden bridge and, immediately afterwards, leave the track in favour of a

If you are on the track early in the morning, keep your eye out for chamois which are often seen here.

path on the left (indicated by red and white waymarks which are followed all the way to the col). Shortly afterwards, arrive at a forest chalet and picnic spot – follow the signs for 'Col des Thures', continuing to head uphill on the path which winds its way N through the trees.

When the path arrives at a track, continue uphill. After another few minutes, at a fork, keep right, heading towards a wooden sign for 'les Thures'. The path soon fords a stream and continues to rise.

After a few minutes pass a strange needle-shaped rock called 'la Demoiselle' ('the fairy chimney'). Shortly afterwards, arrive at a junction of paths with a signpost – turn left in the direction of Col des Thures.

Eventually, arrive at a grassy plateau (1hr 15min). Continue ahead on the same path. At the next signpost, go straight ahead in the direction of Col des Thures. The views to the N begin to open up the closer you get to the col.

The violas on the col in spring are magnificent.

Arrive at **Col des Thures** (2194m, 1hr 45min) and the beautiful **Lac Chavillon**. From here the views both N and S are exceptional. The large triangular pointy mountain to the N is Roche Bernaude. To the NW is Mont Thabor. ◀

From the col, retrace your steps back across the grassy plateau to the S. Approaching the forest at the S side of the plateau, you will arrive at a junction (2hr 15min). Take the left fork (signposted to 'Col de l'Echelle'). To the

The broad Col des Thures with Mont Thabor in the background

The lovely Chapelle Notre Dame de Bon Rencontre

S, on the other side of the Clarée Valley, you can see Fort de l'Olive and Fort Lenlon (Walk 2).

5min from the junction, the path enters the forest and begins to climb. After another 5min or so, ignore a path heading down to the right. Eventually, the path reaches a grassy saddle (2hr 45min) and crosses over to the other side of it. When you arrive at a junction (2hr 50min) with a wooden signpost, turn right (towards 'Plampinet GR57') and descend to the S on another path.

When this path arrives at another junction (3hr 25min), turn right towards Plampinet. Eventually, the path meets a road: descend on the road past the chapel of **Notre Dame de Bon Rencontre**. Keep going down the road for about 1km.

When the road arrives at a track on the right (4hr 5min), with a signpost for 'Forêt Dominale de la Clarée', leave the road and take the track. After a few minutes, ignore another track on the right and keep straight ahead.

The track eventually crosses a bridge and shortly afterwards, arrives at a road (4hr 20min) – turn right and head W up the road. After another 5min arrive back at the car park (4hr 25min).

WALK 4

Lac Noir

Start/finish	Névache (1610m, UTM 32T 311469 4987839)
Distance	12.5km
Ascent/descent	825m
Grade	Hard
Time	4hr 50min
Maximum altitude	2400m
Map	IGN 3535OT Névache (1:25,000)
Refreshments	Restaurants in Névache
Access	From the top of Briançon take the N94 towards Montgenèvre. After about 3km at la Vachette exit onto the D994 and follow this all the way to Névache. Park in the large car park at the tourist office.

If you like lonely places then this is the walk for you. Lac Noir is one of the hardest lakes in the Clarée Valley to access due to the lack of a good path on the final ascent, and this seems to deter the majority of walkers. The route is stunning throughout and the lake itself is divine, set high above the Vallon Valley and surrounded by jagged peaks.

Both navigation and terrain are straightforward, except for the final 45min up to the lake which are difficult. On this section there are few paths and route finding relies largely on cairns that can be hard to spot. In low visibility, therefore, the lake could be difficult to locate.

From the tourist office, walk W through the 'Ville Haute' of Névache. After a few minutes pass to the right of a church and take the road that runs to the left immediately behind it (before the 'Auberge du Clot'). After a few metres, keep straight ahead on the road (signposted 'Col du Vallon') which passes between buildings and soon starts to climb.

Where the village road meets the main route (D301T), turn left and head up the main route to the

W. After 5min the road bends around to the left. Shortly afterwards, leave the road in favour of a path which heads uphill to the right (NW), signposted 'Lac Noir' and 'Col du Vallon'. You will stay on this path almost all the way to Lac Noir.

After about 15min, cross a gully and continue upwards. About 1hr from the start the path levels off and meanders up the Vallon Valley, which is packed with wild flowers in the spring and early summer. Soon the beautifully situated Chapelle St. Michel can be seen above to the N.

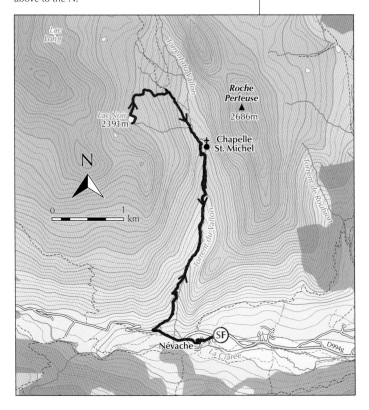

The little hill just up behind the chapel makes a very tranquil rest stop and the views back down the valley to the S are superb.

After 1hr 30min the path starts climbing steeply to arrive at **Chapelle St. Michel** (2123m, 1hr 40min). ◀

From the chapel continue uphill on the path (NW). After 10–15min pass the Chalets du Vallon (2174m) to continue on up the path.

A few minutes after the chalets, leave the path (at coordinates UTM 32T 310931 4991239) to cross grassy slopes to the left in the direction of a cairn on some rocks. Be careful, as the cairn is hard to spot. Then climb SW over the grassy slopes following a series of cairns (which are often difficult to spot).

Soon the cairns start to run towards the NW. Shortly afterwards, pick up a faint path and keep following the cairns (now to the W). When the cairns arrive in front of a rocky outcrop, head up to the S (still following cairns which are again hard to spot).

Chapelle St. Michel with its magnificent outlook over the Vallon Valley

After a few more minutes, pick up a faint path heading W (cairns). Alternatively, you can continue to follow other cairns directly to the S but that route crosses more tricky terrain.

Where the path disappears again, keep heading W towards a scree slope. As you approach the scree slope, bear around to the S (cairns) and follow a faint path S all the way to **Lac Noir** (2391m, 2hr 45min).

From the lake simply retrace your steps to arrive back at **Névache** (4hr 50min).

Mountains reflected in Lac Noir on a still day

WALK 5
Refuge de Buffère by the Côte Rouge

Start/finish	Névache (1610m, UTM 32T 311469 4987839)
Distance	10km
Ascent/descent	620m
Grade	Medium
Time	3hr 50min
Maximum altitude	2157m
Map	IGN 3535OT Névache (1:25,000)
Refreshments	Restaurants in Névache; Refuge de Buffère
Access	From the top of Briançon take the N94 towards Montgenèvre. After about 3km, exit at la Vachette onto the D994 and follow this all the way to Névache. Park in the large car park at the tourist office.

This walk makes for a superb introduction to the Clarée Valley. Starting from the beautifully situated village of Névache, you climb through aromatic larch forest to the Côte Rouge, a fantastic balcony high above the valley floor. The views are exquisite. Afterwards, the Refuge de Buffère is a perfectly tranquil place for a spot of lunch.

The terrain causes few concerns as the walk is on clear paths and tracks, except on the Côte Rouge which is rocky underfoot in places. Navigation is also largely straightforward: however, on the Côte Rouge there are a few places where the path is hard to follow. Fortunately, there are pink waymarks to assist.

From the tourist office, walk W through the 'Haute Ville' of Névache. After a few minutes you will approach a little church. Pass to the right of it and before the 'Auberge du Clot' turn left to pass behind the church. Shortly afterwards, follow the sign for 'Pont de l'Outre'. Cross the bridge over the River Clarée, and almost immediately afterwards take the right fork at a junction towards

'Refuge de Buffère' and head along a track. After a short distance the track becomes a path.

After a few minutes you come to another signpost – turn left in the direction of 'Refuge de Buffère' and 'Lac de Cristol'. The path climbs steadily through the forest and there are frequent pink waymarks on the rocks. After climbing for about 1hr 15min, arrive at a T-junction and a signpost. Turn right in the direction of 'Refuge Buffère par Côte Rouge'.

The path continues to rise through the trees to the N and then descends briefly. As you descend, the views open up to the N and E. This is the start of the **Côte Rouge**. The path now undulates NW across the face of

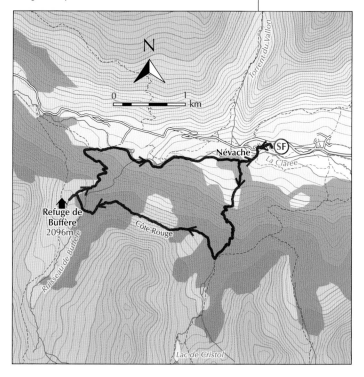

The rust coloured slopes of the Côte Rouge in autumn

The views are spectacular so this is a good place to rest.

the mountain in and out of the trees. The middle section of the Côte Rouge is almost entirely free of trees, perhaps a result of a winter avalanches. ◄

About 2hr 30min from the start arrive at a small wooden footbridge. Cross this and continue ahead on the path. After a few minutes arrive at a track and turn left to reach **Refuge de Buffère** (2096m, 2hr 40min).

> **Refuge de Buffère** is a fine place for lunch or to stay the night. It has 30 dormitory places and is staffed from mid-June until mid-September. Tel +33 (0)4 92 21 34 03, www.refugebuffere.com.

From the refuge retrace your steps downhill. When you reach the path on the right, on which you arrived, keep straight ahead on the track descending to the NE. At the next junction follow the sign for 'Névache' straight ahead. The path reaches the River Clarée and the Pont de Ratley 30min from the refuge. Do not cross this bridge but instead keep straight ahead towards 'Névache'. Keep the river on your left until you arrive back at the Pont de

l'Outre. Retrace your steps across the bridge, through the village and back to the car park.

Refuge de Buffère is a great place to stay or eat

WALK 6

Pic du Lac Blanc, Lac Laramon and Lac du Serpent

Start/finish	Chalets de Fontcouverte (1857m, UTM 32T 306778 4989597)
Distance	14.5km/8.5km for the variation
Ascent/descent	1130m/590m for the variation
Grade	Very hard for the full route (medium to the lakes only)
Time	6hr 15min (variation is 3hr)
Maximum altitude	2980m (variation is 2448m)
Map	IGN 3535OT Névache (1:25,000)
Refreshments	Auberge la Fruitière
Access	From the top of Briançon take the N94 towards Montgenèvre. After about 3km exit at la Vachette onto the D994 and follow this to Névache. Beside the tourist office, take the D301T on the right. After 6km go through the hamlet of Fontcouverte and park on the left before the bridge (beside Auberge la Fruitière). If there are no parking spaces then continue over the bridge and park on the right.

This route visits numerous lakes and climbs a high summit with astonishing views, including a grandstand view of Barre des Écrins and la Meije, in the Écrins National Park, and also Mont Thabor. The ascent to Lacs Laramon and Serpent is straightforward, but after Lac du Serpent the gradients increase and navigation becomes trickier. There's a long traverse of a narrow ridge on the way to the summit, which requires some scrambling, with sheer drops on either side. The descent from the summit is also difficult, involving an extremely steep shale slope. A long section without paths follows, although the terrain itself is not hard.

This walk is not for the novice and is best saved for a fine day. Also, Lacs Laramon and Serpent get very busy in high summer, so start early. The route could easily be shortened to involve only a climb to the Lacs Laramon and Serpent, returning along the same path and avoiding the exposure of the ridge.

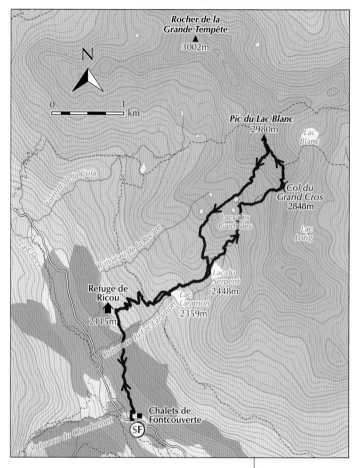

From the road just E of the bridge at Auberge la Fruitière, take a track heading uphill to the NW (signposted 'Lac Laramon and Lac du Serpent'). After 5–10min ignore a track on the right and continue on the main track, generally to the N, all the way to **Refuge de Ricou** (2115m, 40min). ▶

If you start very early, the sunrise on the mountains to the W is magnificent.

Sunrise at Lac Laramon on a still day is very special

Just after the refuge, leave the track in favour of a path on the right (signposted 'Lac Laramon and Lac du Serpent'), which winds its way up the grassy slope. At a junction with signposts, 20–25min after the refuge, follow the track around to the left and continue N (signposted 'Lac Laramon and Lac du Serpent').

Eventually, the path arrives at the magnificent **Lac Laramon** (2359m, 1hr 15min). On a still day the surrounding mountains will be reflected on its surface. The path now makes its way around the N side of the lake and then begins to climb to the N (away from the lake) in the direction of a cairn on a large rock.

Keep climbing to arrive close to **Lac du Serpent** (2448m, 1hr 35min). At a junction of paths before the lake, keep left on a path which heads around the W side of the lake. After heading up to the N of the lake, the path soon begins to climb more steeply and there are cairns which you should follow to ensure that you stay on the correct path.

Eventually, you'll see another lake just below to the W – this is one of the **Lacs des Gardioles**. And shortly afterwards, the second of the Lacs des Gardioles appears on the left. Just at this point the path bends around to the E. Continue, following cairns (particularly where the path disappears), all the way to **Col du Grand Cros** (2848m) where new views to the E present themselves.

At the col, turn left (N) to ascend the ridge all the way to the summit on a steep and rocky path following cairns. Occasionally, the path briefly dips to the W of the ridge and then crests again. When the ridge levels off, continue on the path (now NW). Pic du Lac Blanc can now be clearly seen up above to the NW and the views from the ridge here are spectacular. ▶

The Écrins National Park can be seen to the W including la Meije and Barre des Écrins. Mont Thabor is also clearly visible to the N.

Eventually, the path disappears altogether over rocks – follow the cairns as you scramble along the top of the ridge to attain the summit of **Pic du Lac Blanc** (2980m, 3hr 20min). If you lose the cairns, then just clamber over the rocks to the NW until you reach the summit. Watch your footing here as a fall could have serious consequences.

From the summit, retrace your steps briefly to the SE. Pick up a path that heads initially SE along the W side of

View from the Pic du Lac Blanc

the ridge. Soon this path starts descending a shale slope towards the Lacs des Gardioles to the SW. Watch your footing as the slope is extremely steep and the shale surface does not offer much grip. When the path leaves the shale, crossing large boulders and grass, there are cairns to guide you.

At the bottom of the slope follow cairns through a boulder field to the SW, and shortly afterwards you will see the Lacs des Gardioles below you again. At a cairn on a large rock, pick up a path again which descends towards the closest lake – this rocky slope is very steep.

At the bottom of this slope, follow cairns to head directly to the closest of the lakes. Continue following cairns to head around the S side of this lake and then SW on a path. When the path disappears, simply head down to the next lake (which is visible below) and pass to the right of it.

Then head SW across the grassy slopes in the direction of Barre des Écrins (the highest mountain in the Écrins National Park), which is visible on a clear day. Although there is no path, the grassy terrain is not difficult underfoot.

Eventually, pass between two hillocks and start to descend (still SW) a rocky and grassy slope. Soon a small lake becomes visible below to the S just in front of a large rocky outcrop. Towards the bottom of that slope, you may pick up a faint path and there are some cairns. In any case, head in the direction of the right-hand side of the small lake.

Behind the small lake, pick up a path and follow it to the left. Soon **Lac du Serpent** comes into view again. Follow the path down towards Lac du Serpent and eventually (5hr) arrive at the path travelled earlier. Turn right and descend to **Lac Laramon** (5hr 15min). From here retrace your steps to the start (6hr 15min).

WALK 7
Col des Muandes

Start/finish	Chalets de Laval (2030m, UTM 32T 305209 4992501)
Distance	15.75km
Ascent/descent	945m
Grade	Hard
Time	5hr 45min
Maximum altitude	2828m
Map	IGN 3535OT Névache (1:25,000)
Refreshments	Refuge des Drayères
Access	From the top of Briançon take the N94 towards Montgenèvre. After about 3km take the exit at la Vachette onto the D994 and follow this to Névache. Beside the tourist office, take the D301T right to its end at Chalets de Laval. There is a large car park.

This route is exceptional, taking in three sublime lakes and a magnificent col (facing Mont Thabor), with breathtaking views on all sides. However, such beauty does not give itself up easily. The final ascent to the col is very steep, and although much of the walk is on clear paths, there are a few sections across boulders where care must be taken not to lose the route (cairns and waymarks often assist). In low visibility, or with snow on the ground, the last hour before the col is tricky to navigate and it would be easy to head for the wrong col. In such conditions good map reading and navigation skills are essential. In fine conditions, however, there should be few difficulties. Much of the route is on the GR57 long distance route so there are plenty of red and white waymarks.

From the N side of the car park, take the wide track that runs NW towards Refuge des Drayères. After a minute, at a junction, keep right in the direction of a sign to 'Refuge des Drayères'. Shortly afterwards, at a signpost keep ahead (signposted 'Refuge des Drayères').

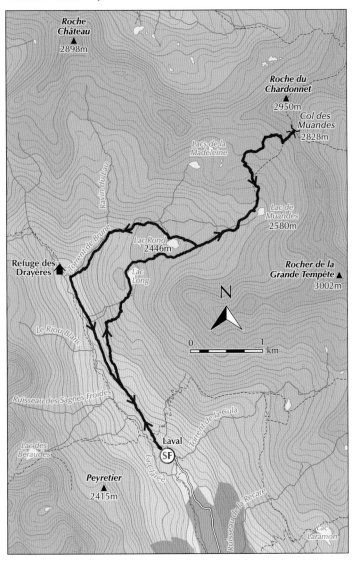

Arriving at another yellow signpost, 15–20min from the start, take the path heading up to the right (signposted 'Col des Muandes'). After another 20min, at a large cairn, the path bends around to the right (E).

The Massif des Cerces as seen from Lac Rond

Keep following the path all the way to **Lac Long** (2387m, 1hr). The path proceeds around the W and N sides of the lake and then climbs to the E.

At a junction of paths, keep right to take the path that runs around the S side of Lac Rond. The path soon proceeds across a rocky plateau. Snow can lie here until early summer which can make locating the path a little tricky, but fortunately there are cairns to guide you. Soon **Lac Rond** can be seen path below on the left (1hr 30min).

After Lac Rond the path heads to the NE across a grassy plateau, crossing a river and a couple of streams. There is also a boulder field where the path disappears so you will need to rely on the cairns and red and white waymarks. Eventually the path arrives at **Lac des Muandes** (2580m, 2hr 15min), charmingly situated in a little mountain cirque.

From this lake follow the path towards the N for a while. The path heads briefly NW as it makes its way to the left of a rocky outcrop, then heads NE to climb across

71

Spectacular views await you at Col des Muandes. Snow is possible here, even in the summer

The views on both sides of the col are fabulous and Mont Thabor sits right in front of you to the NE.

the slopes towards a long ridge of mountains. At a couple of cairns on some level terrain just before the final ascent to the col, head N briefly to start climbing a steep slope (with cairns and red and white waymarks). Then follow the path NE again as it ascends to **Col des Muandes** (2828m, 3hr). ◄

From the col, retrace your steps back to **Lac des Muandes** (3hr 55min). Then head back towards Lac Rond. At the boulder field, follow the waymarks and cairns again. When the path arrives at a junction of paths with a cairn, turn right to take a path heading NW which runs all the way to the N edge of **Lac Rond** (2446m, 4hr 20min).

Immediately after crossing the river that flows out of the N side of the lake, turn right (red and white waymarks) on a path which heads initially NW. Follow the red and white waymarks all the way down to Pont de Pierre, just beside **Refuge des Drayères** (2180m, 5hr 10min).

At the bridge, turn left and take a wide track (signposted 'Refuge de Laval'), descending a magnificent part of the Clarée Valley to arrive back at the car park (5hr 45min).

WALK 8

Tour of the Massif des Cerces

Start/finish	Chalets de Laval (2030m, UTM 32T 305209 4992501)
Distance	18km
Ascent/descent	1050m
Grade	Very hard
Time	6hr 45min
Maximum altitude	2788m
Map	IGN 3535OT Névache (1:25,000)
Refreshments	Refuge des Drayères
Access	From the top of Briançon take the N94 towards Montgenèvre. After about 3km take the exit at la Vachette onto the D994 and follow this to Névache. Beside the tourist office, take the D301T on the right and follow it to its end at Laval. There is a large car park
Warning	This walk contains sections of scrambling and great vertical exposure – not recommended for the inexperienced or in bad weather.

This circuit takes you on a tour of the Massif des Cerces. It is a long, hard route but there is stunning scenery throughout. There are three cols to pass over and at each crossing a new part of this amazing region is presented. The route also takes in seven lovely lakes, any one of which on its own would make a fantastic destination for a hike. Provided you have the skills and experience, this route should not be missed.

The climb to Col des Béraudes is hard. It is very steep from the start, giving your legs no time to warm up. In particular, the section between Lac des Béraudes and Col des Béraudes is very tough – the path is largely made up of shale and is extremely steep in places. The exposure throughout this section is great and a fall could have serious consequences. There is also a section just before the Col des Béraudes where fixed cables are provided to enable you to scramble up. The first part of the descent from Col des Béraudes is also very steep and requires some light scrambling. Needless to say, this is not really a walk for beginners and it would be unwise to attempt it in bad weather.

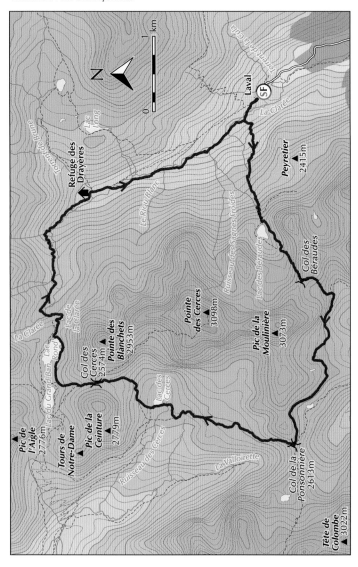

From the N side of the car park, take the wide track that runs NW towards Refuge des Drayères. After a minute, turn left at a junction onto a path (signposted 'Lac des Béraudes'). The path descends to the river and crosses a bridge. Then follow a grassy path NW towards a signpost.

At the signpost, turn left to follow a path uphill (signposted 'Lac des Béraudes'). Straight away the path is very steep. There are occasional yellow waymarks on the rocks. After 20–25min, the path fords a couple of streams and continues relentlessly uphill to arrive at **Lac des Béraudes** (2504m, 1hr 10min). This beautiful dark green lake is set in a rocky mountain bowl surrounded by steep mountains.

Immediately before the lake, turn left (SE) and follow a path heading up around the S side of the lake. This challenging rocky path climbs all the way to the col and is very steep in places. ▶

After 10–15min the path skirts the precipitous edge of a shale slope. Watch your footing here as a fall could

There are plenty of chamois and bouquetin in this area. If you are on the trail early, you may be lucky enough to see one.

The descent from Col des Béraudes – L'Aiguillette du Lauzet and les Arêtes de la Bruyère can be seen on the left (Walks 37 and 38)

have serious consequences. When the path becomes faint in places, keep on the lookout for cairns.

The final part of the climb before the col is very tough. Just below the col, there is a very steep section with a cable to enable you to scramble up. Shortly afterwards, arrive at the **Col des Béraudes** (2hr). ◄

The col may be small but the views are not – to the S most of the highest mountains of the Écrins National Park can be clearly seen.

At the col, turn left (SE) along a little path which soon starts to descend very steeply – at times you will need to scramble down so take care. Soon the gradient decreases but the path still descends fairly steeply.

20–25min from the col, arrive at a junction of paths just before a rocky outcrop – turn left and continue descending. Shortly afterwards, arrive at another junction – turn right to follow a path which heads W towards your next col.

The path contours around the hillside for quite some time. Eventually, at a right-hand bend, a number of lakes come into view, including Grand Lac (S). The lake furthest N is the Lac de la Ponsonnière and your next destination, Col de la Ponsonnière, can be seen up behind the lake.

Keep on the same path past Lac de la Ponsonnière (far below you) and then contour around the hillside all the way to **Col de la Ponsonnière** (2613m, 3hr 20min).

From the col, take the path to the NE running down the right-hand side of the valley. Eventually, the path makes its way across a grassy plateau. When, finally, Lac des Cerces comes into sight, turn right at a junction on a path to head directly towards the lake (NE). Arrive at **Lac des Cerces** (2410m, 4hr) and follow the path around the W side of the lake.

Just past the lake keep on the path as it bends round to the NE and begins to climb. Shortly after the path bends round to the N, it splits – you can take either path as they both converge after a few minutes. Eventually, the gradient levels off and you continue to the N to reach **Col des Cerces** (2574m, 4hr 30min).

From the col keep heading N on a path (signposted 'Refuge des Drayères') and, almost immediately, another lake comes into view. Just 5min from the col, arrive at a junction of paths and keep right (signposted to three lakes). After a few more minutes, the path disappears briefly over rocky terrain – follow the cairns until you pick the path up again.

Soon you arrive above the **Lac du Grand Ban**. Here the path splits – keep right to head around the S side of **Lac Rond** (2450m). At the E side of Lac Rond, the path proceeds through a boulder field: follow cairns and red and white waymarks to head NE around the edge of the lake.

When the path arrives onto the grass again, keep straight ahead and shortly afterwards arrive at a wide path. Turn right, and after a few minutes yet another lake comes into view. Follow the wide path down to the edge of the turquoise **Lac de la Clarée** (2433m).

Cross the river flowing out of the lake and imme-diately afterwards, turn left on a path heading initially N. Follow the red and white waymarks, ignore any off-shoots and keep on the main path to arrive at **Refuge des Drayères** (2180m, 5hr 55min).

Descend to the left of the refuge on a track (sign-posted 'Refuge de Laval'). The track soon arrives at the

The magnificent Clarée Valley in autumn

On the descent from Col de la Ponsonnière

In the autumn, the trees here are resplendent with colour.

river and crosses a bridge. After the bridge, keep ahead (S) on the track (signposted 'Refuge de Laval').

After a few minutes, at a signpost, leave the track in favour of a path on the right (signposted 'Refuge de Laval (par la rive droite)'). Shortly afterwards, cross a bridge and continue on a path to the S. ◄ The path undulates as it makes its way generally downriver. In a grassy meadow, where the path splits, you can go either left or right. The path also fords a few streams – be careful here in the spring when there is a lot of water.

Eventually, the path arrives at the signpost you passed earlier – turn left, cross the bridge and head up the path back to the car park (6hr 45min).

Mont Chaberton is one of the finest viewpoints in the Briançonnais (Walk 11)

MONTGENÈVRE

WALK 9

Le Chenaillet

Start/finish	Base of the Chalmettes ski lift, Montgenèvre (1840m, UTM 32T 320013 4977564)
Distance	13km
Ascent/descent	895m
Grade	Hard
Time	5hr 10min
Maximum altitude	2650m
Map	IGN 3536OT Briançon (1:25,000)
Refreshments	Montgenèvre
Access	From Briançon head NE on the N94 to Montgenèvre. At the first roundabout turn right towards 'les Chalmettes'. Almost immediately afterwards, turn left onto a small road where there is a parking area on the left.

Le Chenaillet is a highlight of the Montgenèvre area, with far-reaching 360° views of the Briançonnais and also into Italy from its rocky summit. The route ascends through an aromatic larch forest and beautiful alpine pastures, before a fascinating and somewhat exposed geological path brings you to the summit. There is also an easier, scramble-free option.

Navigation and terrain are relatively straightforward. Part of the walk passes through ski slopes but this is hardly a blot on the landscape: Montgenèvre has escaped much of the degradation and scarring that afflict many larger French ski resorts. There may be a couple of ski lifts here and there but the stunning scenery remains largely pristine.

Walk SW on the small road in the direction of a ski lift. At a signpost under another ski lift, turn left in the direction of 'le Chenaillet' and begin to climb up a gravel track roughly in line with the ski lift. After a few minutes, turn right at a fork onto a path signposted towards 'le Chenaillet'.

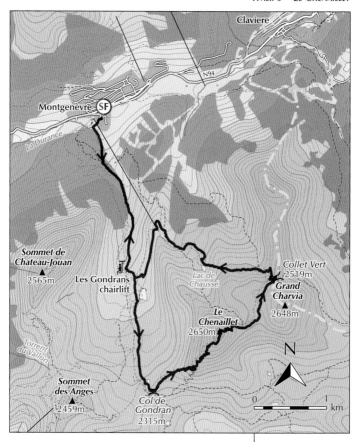

At a junction, ignore the post directing you to the left and keep straight ahead. Cross a stream and keep on climbing through the larch forest. Soon the path meets a mountain bike track: turn left and keep on the path to the left, rather than the mountain bike track. ▶ After a few minutes, where the path arrives at a junction of tracks, keep straight ahead (S).

Watch out for mountain bikes as they go pretty fast.

81

Mont Chaberton as seen from the track to Col du Gondran

Shortly afterwards, turn right onto a path signposted towards 'le Chenaillet'. Eventually, the path rises steeply to meet another track. Turn right and head up this track. Shortly afterwards, ignore another track heading up to your right and keep ahead on the main track.

After 5min or so, leave the track and bear left on a path signposted to 'le Chenaillet'. At the bottom of the **les Gondrans chairlift** turn left and take one of the paths heading uphill to the SE. Ignore any tracks to the E. Soon you will see a wooden building in front of you. At a signpost before the wooden building head S up a track (signposted to 'le Chenaillet'). After a few minutes, bear left along a path which runs alongside the track and head towards a signpost up ahead.

From the signpost continue to climb to the S (signposted to 'le Chenaillet'). At a junction of three paths, take the left branch up a grassy path. The route now heads across grassy pastures. The summit of le Chenaillet is the dominating peak above on the left. At a junction, leave the main path in favour of a grassy path on the left. After a few minutes, aim towards a signpost up ahead of you.

The **Col de Gondran** (2315m) is reached about 1hr 30min from the start. Take the path to the left and descend briefly to the Cabane de Douaniers. Turn left at another signpost to 'le Chenaillet' and head upwards on the 'sentier géologique'. The path leads you up across the top of the ridge.

This area displays some interesting **geology**. The path marks the boundary between the oceanic crust and mantle rocks, and information boards point out the different types of rock.

Descend briefly and arrive at a junction of paths. Here you have two options: head to the left to take the steeper, more direct, path straight up the mountain (the *direttissimo*, as the Italians would say). Alternatively, you can turn to the right and take a slightly easier, and more circuitous, path which winds its way up the S face of the mountain. Both of these paths converge before the summit. The views to the N are better on the direct route.

View from the summit of le Chenaillet

As you get higher the **views** to the S into the Cerveyrette Valley get better and better. You can also see the road up to the famous cycling col, the Col d'Izoard. To the SW is the Écrins National Park.

The 360° views are out of this world on a fine day. To the N, you should clearly see Mont Chaberton (Walk 11).

The summit of **le Chenaillet** (2650m) is reached about 2hr 40min from the start. ◄

To descend, take the path to the E of the summit towards Collet Vert. As you descend, you may hear the shrill cries of the many marmots. A steep section of the path is protected by a steel cable. At a junction of paths on a small saddle, 10–15min from the summit, take the path to the right and head over a small rise. Keep following the path down the other side. Soon the path bears left and heads in a generally N direction. After a few minutes, at a crossroads, keep straight ahead to pass underneath a chairlift.

Notice the fort of le Janus on the mountain up ahead of you.

Soon afterwards, arrive at **Collet Vert** (2519m), 3hr 20min from the start. The views into Italy are fantastic. Take the path to the W of the col and descend on a rocky path with some steep sections. At a junction take the left fork towards 'Lac de Chaussé'. ◄

After 3hr 50min arrive at **Lac de Chaussé** (2287m), where le Chenaillet towers above you. Just to the north of the lake you will find a track: turn right towards a chairlift and descend. At the bottom of the Rocher de l'Aigle chairlift, take the track that heads uphill to the NW. After a few minutes, this bears to the left and heads S back to the **les Gondrans chairlift**. From here, descend on the route climbed earlier to arrive back at the start (5hr 10min).

WALK 10
Fort du Gondran

Start/finish	Base of the Chalmettes ski lift, Montgenèvre (1840m, UTM 32T 320013 4977564)
Distance	11.5km
Ascent/descent	638m
Grade	Medium
Time	3hr 30min
Maximum altitude	2459m
Map	IGN 3536OT Briançon (1:25,000)
Refreshments	Montgenèvre
Access	From Briançon head NE on the N94 to Montgenèvre. At the first roundabout turn right towards 'les Chalmettes'. Almost immediately afterwards, turn left onto a small road where you will see a parking area on the left.

This lovely walk climbs from Montgenèvre to a grassy col, with superb views into the Cerveyrette Valley, then along a high ridge topped by a historic fort and many other interesting military buildings. It is not a terribly difficult walk but the views are magnificent and the myriad of military buildings make this an ideal outing for history buffs.

The terrain is straightforward throughout, with the route following clear tracks and paths, but Montgenèvre and its surrounds have a labyrinth of tracks and paths which can often be confusing – pay close attention to the walk description and follow your progress on the IGN map.

Initially walk SW on the small road in the direction of a ski lift. At a signpost under another ski lift, turn left in the direction of 'le Chenaillet' and begin to climb up a gravel track roughly in line with the ski lift. After a few minutes, turn right at a fork onto a path signposted towards 'le Chenaillet'.

After a few more minutes, at a wooden post with a yellow waymark indicating a left-hand turn, leave the path in favour of another path on the left heading uphill to the NE – this path is easy to miss. After a few metres the path splits – turn right and ascend to the SE.

After 15min the path passes under a chairlift and arrives at a junction of tracks – turn right here and briefly descend on a gravel track heading down to the S towards the trees. Do not take the gravel track heading to the SE parallel to a chair lift.

Shortly after entering the trees, immediately before a stream, turn left on a path signposted 'le Chenaillet'. Keep on this path, climbing gently alongside the stream, until the path finally rises more steeply and arrives at a track (35min). Head up the track to the SE. After a few minutes, ignore a track rising from the right and keep ahead.

After 5min or so, leave the track and bear left on a path signposted to 'le Chenaillet'. When you arrive at the bottom of the **les Gondrans chairlift**, turn left and take one of the paths heading uphill to the SE. Ignore any tracks to the E. Soon you will see a wooden building in front of you. Arrive at a signpost before the wooden building and head S up a track (signposted to 'le Chenaillet'). After a few minutes, bear left along a path which runs alongside the track and head towards a signpost up ahead. ◄

Beside the signpost there is a very interesting display on the geology of the region.

From the signpost continue to climb to the S (signposted to 'le Chenaillet'). At a junction of three paths, take the left branch up a grassy path. The route now heads across grassy pastures. The summit of le Chenaillet is the dominating peak above on the left. At a junction leave the main path in favour of a grassy path on the left.

After a few minutes, aim towards a signpost up ahead to arrive at **Col de Gondran** (2315m, 1hr 30min).

> For a **fine viewpoint** continue straight ahead at the crossroads to climb a small rise on a little rocky path. The views into the Cerveyrette Valley are fantastic.

From the col, head SW along the ridge on a faint path. After a few minutes join a track which heads S and then SW. Keep on this track until (after a few minutes) it

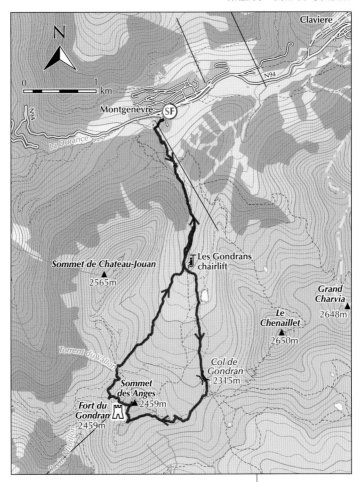

slips in behind the ridge. Here, you can either keep on the track or you can branch off left on a faint path and keep to the crest of the ridge: the latter option preserves the views better, and you will pick up the track again in a few minutes in any case.

Fort du Gondran is well preserved and stunningly situated

From here, Fort Janus can be seen to the N and Fort de l'Infernet to the W.

Arrive back at the track in front of a small hill with paths running around it in either direction. Take the path on the right-hand side, which has some interesting geological structures with boards explaining them. After a few minutes, arrive back at the track again where you will find the first military buildings of the day. Keep on the track, heading W. When you eventually meet another track, turn right and head up the track to the N for 5min or so to reach **Fort du Gondran** (2459m, 2hr). ◄

From Fort du Gondran, retrace your steps briefly back down the track until you come to grassy track on the right. Take this grassy track, which descends through a variety of fascinating military buildings that you can explore at your leisure.

The grassy track winds its way back and forth down the hillside (W): aim for a junction of gravel tracks just below. When you arrive at the junction (2hr 15min; coordinates UTM 32T 319116 4973784) take the track to the right (N). After a few minutes the track passes between more military buildings.

FORT DU GONDRAN

Parts A to D were built between 1876 and 1910 to protect Briançon from invasion across Col de Montgenèvre or through the Cerveyrette Valley. Part E was constructed between 1935 and 1939 as part of the Maginot Line (named after the then French Minister of War, André Maginot), a defensive line of fortifications to protect France's E borders against a German or Italian invasion.

The fortifications extend for approximately 1800m along a ridge overlooking Montgenèvre to the N and the Cerveyrette Valley to the S. There were 16 batteries of four guns each and a garrison of about 800 men. The buildings offer an insight into the tough conditions soldiers here must have faced.

Military installations include bunkers, barracks and magazines. It is possible to enter many of these but be careful for some are in a state of disrepair and could be dangerous.

At a junction of tracks beside a little stone bridge, turn right. After a few more minutes arrive at another junction of tracks (where there is a monument to France's military dead in Algeria). Turn right on a track. Although there is a sign for Montgenèvre at this junction, the sign is pointing in the wrong direction so be careful.

The stunning vista that awaits you on the descent from Fort du Gondran

As you proceed along this path, Mont Chaberton (Walk 11) stands tall in front of you.

After a few metres, where the track bends round to the right, leave the track for a small grassy path (which is easy to miss) heading NE (coordinates UTM 32T 319280 4974217). Keep your eyes peeled because the path is faint in a few places. ◄

Eventually the path leads back down again to the base of the **les Gondrans chairlift** (3hr). From here, retrace your steps back to the start (3hr 30min).

Mont Chaberton is the dominant feature as you descend back into the valley

WALK 11

Mont Chaberton

Start/finish	Montgenèvre Office de Tourisme (1850m, UTM 32T 320659 4977977)
Distance	17.5km
Ascent/descent	1295m
Grade	Very hard
Time	6hr 40min
Maximum altitude	3131m
Map	IGN 3536OT Briançon (1:25,000)
Refreshments	Montgenèvre
Access	From Briançon, head NE on the N94 to Montgenèvre. At the first roundabout, go straight ahead and pass through a tunnel. At a roundabout with an obelisk beside it, turn left and pass the tourist office on your right. Then turn left to enter a car park.

This 3131m peak is perhaps the finest single viewpoint in the whole of the region. From the top, on a clear day you can see for miles in every direction – even Mont Blanc can be seen to the N. This difficult walk is a must for those wanting a challenge.

Route finding does not pose many difficulties – the first hour of the walk is on the GR5 long distance route, so there are plenty of red and white waymarks. After leaving the GR5, there are yellow or pink waymarks all the way to the summit. The ascent beyond the GR5 is steep and rocky, especially the section before Col du Chaberton. The maximum altitude on this route is high, so save this walk for a fine day. It is also best to start early in the morning, to avoid the worst of the midday heat.

From the car park, head back along the road towards the roundabout (with the obelisk) and then continue NE on a footpath at the side of the road (N94). You are on the GR5, so for the next hour follow red and white waymarks.

The route passes through this beautiful valley both on the ascent and the descent

About 5min from the start, turn left onto a path. Keep on the path for a few minutes until it meets a road: from here continue NE on the path running alongside the road.

When the path joins the road again, keep uphill to the NE on the road. Shortly afterwards, leave the road for a track on the left, again heading uphill to the NE (signposted 'Mont Chaberton GR5'). Soon the track bears to the N and continues to climb. Keep on this track following red and white waymarks.

Mont Chaberton can be seen above to the right.

After 35–40min leave the track in favour of a path on the left. ◄ After a few more minutes, the path meets the track again: keep ahead uphill (N).

Arriving at a junction with a signpost (1hr) keep right (signposted 'Mont Chaberton GR5') to leave the track in favour of a path. The path splits a few times: just keep following the red and white waymarks.

When the path arrives at a grassy plateau, you will see a signpost up ahead. At the signpost, leave the GR5 and keep ahead on a track to the N towards the base of a chairlift. After a few more minutes, leave the track in favour of a path on the right (signposted 'le Chaberton') to head across a river bed and proceed N across the grassy

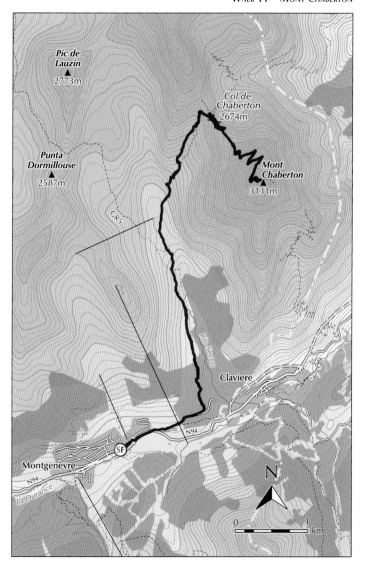

Mont Chaberton as seen from the summit of le Chenaillet

plain on the other side. Now there are waymarks in a variety of colours (most commonly yellow or pink) all the way to the summit.

Soon the path starts to climb steeply up the right flank of the valley. At an information board, the path heads steeply up to the NE towards Col du Chaberton, which can be seen above.

After 10–15min, the path crosses a ravine and continues relentlessly upwards on the other side. Eventually, the path passes back over to the right-hand side of the ravine. Finally, the path bears around to the E and continues upwards to arrive at **Col du Chaberton** (2674m, 2hr 40min), where there is an information board. The Italian border is about 1km to the E of the col.

At the col, turn right (SE) and continue to climb. There is a variety of paths and tracks you can take up to the summit: some are steeper than others, and if in doubt just follow the waymarks. ▸

Finally, after a long hard climb, arrive at the summit of **Mont Chaberton** (3131m, 4hr).

From the **summit** you overlook the entire region: the Mercantour to the S, the whole of the Écrins National Park to the W, and the Vanoise and the Gran Paradiso National Park both to the N, are all

Abandoned barbed wire bears witness to the military history of this place: indeed the tracks themselves are old military roads.

FORT DU CHABERTON

Mont Chaberton was part of Italy until after the Second World War. The fort on the summit was built between 1891 and 1914 by the Italians, who cut away the top of the mountain (reducing it by about 6m) to seat a battery of eight 149mm guns. They also built a road all the way from the Susa Valley to the summit to supply the fort.

The guns were removed during First World War to be used on the Austrian frontier and the fort had to be re-armed by Benito Mussolini in the 1930s. In 1940 the fort garrisoned 320 soldiers, but that summer French mortars destroyed most of the guns and neutralised the fort. After the end of the war France acquired the mountain and the border was relocated to the village of Claviere.

Gun emplacements at the summit of Mont Chaberton

visible. However, most excitingly, Mont Blanc is visible to the N on a clear day. You will want to spend some time here.

There are a number of gun emplacements on the summit which should keep the history buffs happy. To help identify the many peaks that can be seen, there are fantastic information boards all around the summit.

When you have managed to drag yourself away from the col, descend on the same path back to **Col du Chaberton**. From here, turn left and retrace your steps back to Montgenèvre (6hr 40min).

On the descent, keep following the waymarks and shortly after leaving the col, be careful not to miss the slight right turn to cross to the right-hand side of the gorge. There is a path that runs all the way down the left-hand side of the gorge but it is more difficult.

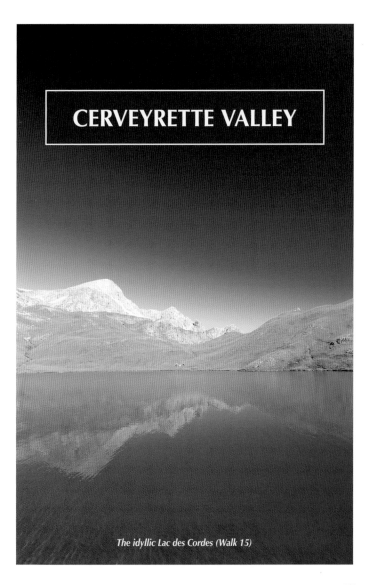

CERVEYRETTE VALLEY

The idyllic Lac des Cordes (Walk 15)

WALK 12
Alp du Pied

Start/finish	Eglise St-Michel at the top of the village of Cervières (1640m, UTM 32T 319813 4971073)
Distance	3.75km
Ascent/descent	280m
Grade	Easy
Time	1hr 45min
Maximum altitude	1915m
Map	IGN 3536OT Briançon (1:25,000)
Refreshments	Cervières
Access	From the bottom of the hill below Briançon's old town, follow signs for the Col d'Izoard onto the D902 towards Cervières. At Cervières turn left (signposted 'les Fonts'). Shortly afterwards turn left again, crossing a bridge over a river, and head NE. Soon after, turn left again, signposted 'les Fonts' and 'Eglise St-Michel'. Head uphill and park at a small lay-by at the apex of a hairpin bend below Eglise St-Michel. There are two churches in Cervières: St-Michel is the one at the top of the village, not down by the river.

This fantastic little walk demonstrates how easy it can be to get up into the high mountains. A straightforward climb brings you to the pretty hamlet of l'Alpe du Pied and then a stunning alpine pasture with great views of the Cerveyrette Valley and the Écrins National Park. The walk can be extended slightly by adding a short ascent up to the buildings of L'Alpe de Guion. Navigation poses few difficulties, save for the faint paths in and around the pasture.

From the lay-by take the path heading N (signposted 'Chalet de l'Alpe'), passing to the left of the church. The path initially skirts a ravine with some interesting rock formations. After 5–10min cross a wooden foot bridge, then turn either left or right: both paths come back together after a few minutes, although the path to the right is probably a little less steep.

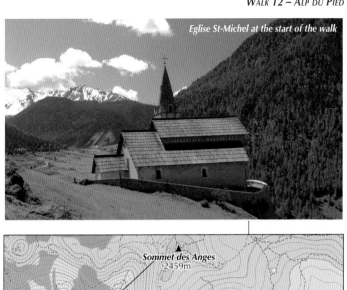

Eglise St-Michel at the start of the walk

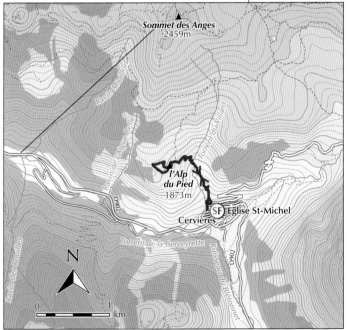

Sommet des Anges
2459m

Ravin Mhaflon

Ravin de l'agne belle

Torrent du Villard

l'Alp
du Pied
1873m

D902

SF Eglise St-Michel

Cervières

Ravin des Reallles

Torrent de-la-Cerveyrette

Ruisseau du Bletonnet

D902

N

0   1
km

About 20min from the start the path tops a small rise and then descends briefly through trees towards a stream (which may be dry in the summer). Cross the stream and climb again on the path, to arrive at **l'Alpe du Pied** (1873m, 40min), a small hamlet with a little church. To find a superb view point, walk a couple minutes SE from the hamlet towards an old ruin with a cross next to it.

Here, in spring, you may be lucky enough to hear the call of the area's many cuckoos.

To continue with the route, pass to the left of the hamlet and the fountain and follow a small track W. ◀

After a few minutes the path bends to the left and continues uphill, passing to the left of an old ruin and bending around to the right behind it. From here, keep SW along the path skirting the edges of a high alpine pasture.

Soon the path arrives at a stone farm building: bear right (W), keeping just to the right of the building and heading along some grassy terraces.

The pasture would make a fantastic picnic spot, with views of the Écrins National Park (visible to the W).

After a few minutes the grassy terraces arrive at a crossroad of faint paths (coordinates UTM 32T 319057 4971698). Turn right (E) and head across the pasture on a faint track back in the direction of l'Alpe du Pied. The path is very faint in places but just keep heading E across the pasture until you see l'Alpe du Pied. ◀

As you cross the pasture, you will also notice the buildings of l'Alpe de Guion above to the left. Should you wish to extend this short walk a little, you can climb the grassy slopes up to the buildings.

You are sure to hear cow bells at l'Alp du Pied

From the pasture head back down to **l'Alpe du Pied** and then retrace your steps to **Cervières** (1hr 45min).

WALK 13
Fort de la Lausette and the Peygus

Start/finish	Le Laus (1745m, UTM 32T 320305 4969630)
Distance	14.5km
Ascent/descent	1070m
Grade	Very hard
Time	6hr 10min
Maximum altitude	2612m
Map	IGN 3536OT Briançon (1:25,000)
Refreshments	Le Laus
Access	From the bottom of the hill below Briançon's old town, follow signs for the Col d'Izoard onto the D902 towards Cervières. Pass Cervières, in the direction of Col d'Izoard, and after 2km reach le Laus, where there is a parking area on the left over a little bridge. Alternatively, there is parking a few hundred metres before le Laus on the right.

It does not get much better than this one: an ancient military fort perched on a ledge, a challenging climb to a high mountain col, an emerald lake and stunning alpine pastures. The climb to the col is very steep, on loose shale, so care needs to be taken.

From either parking area, walk S along the D902. A few hundred metres past the village, you will find a little cabin on the right where the road bends to the left. From the cabin, follow the track that heads up across the face of the slope in a NW direction (signposted to 'Fort de la Lausette'). Soon after, at a fork, keep right to follow a path: yellow waymarks on the trees assist with navigation. Soon the path gets rocky and begins to climb more steeply out of the trees. The path heads up into a cleft in the cliffs to the NW: from time to time you should see

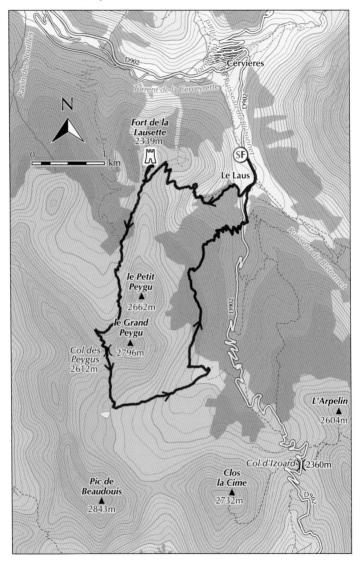

more yellow flashes on the rocks to guide you. To the SW le Grand Peygu stands proud.

The view N from Fort de la Lausette

After 1hr 5min the path enters a grassy valley. Up ahead, on the left, the Fort de la Lausette perches on the rocks. At a signpost for 'les Chalets d'Izoard', turn right and climb to the N. Where the path bears left, ignore another path heading straight ahead. Eventually the path meets a wide track: turn left onto this track.

At a junction of paths on a broad saddle, turn right and climb any one of the paths heading uphill to arrive at the **Fort de la Lausette** (2339m, 1hr 30min). ▶

To the SE the Col d'Izoard (of Tour de France fame) can be clearly seen.

Built between 1887 and 1889, **Fort de la Lausette** was used as an observation post for neighbouring batteries. The fort garrisoned 50–80 infantry soldiers and protected Briançon from an infantry assault from Italy or across the Col d'Izoard.

From the fort, head back down the hill, the way you came, to reach the saddle. Keep straight ahead (S) on a track. Soon the path starts to descend. Far ahead of you is

The view N from Col de Peygus

the Col de Peygus (your next destination). After descending on this track for 5–10min, leave the track where it bends round to the right in favour of a path heading uphill to the left. ◄ Keep on this path all the way to the col.

Be careful not to miss this path, as there are no signposts.

As you climb, you will see your path far ahead, snaking up to the col. Eventually this path crosses a slope covered with shale: it is fairly challenging, so watch your step. Soon the path begins to climb very steeply up the face of the shale slope to the col: at times it is a case of two steps forward and one step back. You need to take care here as a fall could have serious consequences.

Arrive at **Col de Peygus** (2612m, 3hr). From here, descend to the S, heading for a path on the right-hand side of a crag (which you should see downhill on the left). Soon you should see below a little **turquoise lake** (2392m), not named on the IGN map. You should arrive at the lake after about 3hr 40min.

From the lake, head E on a faint path, heading down through the grassy hillocks. Eventually the path peters out: keep heading E down the grassy slopes towards the Chalets d'Izoard, which you should see in front of you.

Descend the crest of a grassy spur and at the bottom of it, cross over a stream. On the other side of the stream continue to head E towards the Chalets d'Izoard. ▸

There is no path but the terrain is easy.

At a dilapidated chalet with a cross (before the new chalet up ahead) head NW back towards the stream. Cross over and pick up a path heading diagonally up the hill on the W side of the stream. The path initially heads W across the face of the slope and shortly afterwards turns to the N. The path climbs for about 10–15min and towards the end of the climb it enters a forest. There are now yellow waymarks on the rocks to guide you. The forest, which is not too dense, provides beautiful views to the E.

After another 20min arrive at a fork (at coordinates UTM 32T 319414 4968109). It is easy to miss, but yellow waymarks on a rock and a small cairn in the fork itself help to locate it. Take the right-hand fork and follow the path downhill (guided by more yellow waymarks).

Arrive at the main road 5hr 45min from the start. Cross the road and immediately head down a bank on the other side towards a stream. There is no path here and it seems a bit of a pain having to descend the bank, but the alternative is to walk down the main road for 1km. Cross the stream and turn left, following its direction. Almost immediately, you'll see a sign to the NE for 'Sentier Botanique'. Briefly head towards the sign and come to a path. Follow the path downhill towards the stream (not uphill, in the direction of the Sentier Botanique). Keep following this path all the way back to **le Laus** (6hr 10min).

WALK 14

Col de Bousson

Start/finish	The chapel at le Bourget (1872m, UTM 32T 324090 4971387)
Distance	6.75km
Ascent/descent	340m
Grade	Easy
Time	2hr 10min
Maximum altitude	2170m
Map	IGN 3536OT Briançon (1:25,000)
Refreshments	None
Access	From the bottom of the hill below Briançon's old town, follow signs for the Col d'Izoard onto the D902 towards Cervières. At Cervières, turn left (signposted 'les Fonts'). Keep following the signs for les Fonts until you arrive at the hamlet of le Bourget. Park either on the grass in front of the chapel on the W side of le Bourget or at the side of the road (D89T) near the chapel.

For a short walk with little height gain this one really packs a punch. It explores a lovely part of the quiet and remote Cerveyrette Valley and takes you well above 2000m. The views are spectacular. It also crosses over into Italy (albeit briefly). Although this walk is graded 'easy', be aware that in low visibility it would be easy to lose your way on and around the indistinct Col de Bousson.

Pass to the right of the chapel and take the path to the left immediately behind it (NW). After about 5min, at a group of buildings known as les Hugues on the IGN map, keep straight ahead along a track signposted to 'Col de Bousson'. This track runs almost all the way to the col.

At **Rif Tord** (1902m) take the right fork steeply uphill. The track winds its way up through grassy slopes.

Be sure to listen for the shrill whistles of **marmots**, for there are many to be seen here. The slopes are usually a verdant green in early summer: in autumn they are a glorious golden brown.

Pass an old *cabane de douaniers* (customs office) on your right and, shortly afterwards, a bergerie and two

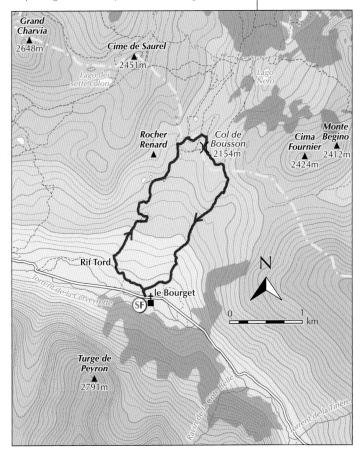

About 5min after the bergerie the track becomes faint in places.

small lakes. The path bends round to the left behind the bergerie. At the second lake, ignore the small paths to the right and keep ahead on the main track. ◄ The track continues to climb and passes to the E of the **Rocher Renard**.

After the Rocher Renard, at a signpost beside a lake, the left fork is signposted towards Col de Bousson. Be aware that although this signpost indicates that the Col de Bousson is only 5mins away, it is in fact more like 15–20mins and is relatively difficult to pinpoint. It is possible to reach the col by taking the right fork at the sign – indeed this is the most direct route – but the left fork takes you on a slightly longer, more scenic route and is the route that is described here.

A few minutes after taking the left fork, take a path to the right (ignoring the track straight ahead). After a few minutes you will see a lake ahead of you as you pass between two small hills to left and right. Ignore both the track ahead (towards the lake) and the track to the left (which takes you to Borne Frontière 31.1). The Bornes Frontières are stone border markers on the frontier between France and Italy. Instead, turn right (E) up a

The stone marker at Col de Bousson

The chapel at Bourget

small rise and follow the frontier in a roughly E direction (over the tops of the grassy hillocks). Note that there is no path in places but if you use the Bornes Frontières to guide you then you will not go far wrong – look carefully for these as they are sometimes hard to spot. The numbers on the Bornes Frontières increase the further E you get.

Follow the frontier as it snakes back and forth (broadly E) across the tops of the hillocks until you descend slightly to arrive at Borne Frontière 32 (2154m) just over 1hr from the start of the walk. On the IGN map, the **Col de Bousson** (2154m) is marked just below this point to the S. At the col there are stunning views to the S towards the Turge de Peyron and the Cime de la Charvie.

From the col take the path heading towards the SE. ▶ The path veers E and then towards the S, arriving at Borne Frontière 33.1 about 5min from the col. Keep on the path to the S (crossing back into France) and ignore a track heading up to the left. The path heads SE and then SW, then becomes a track which descends a broad grassy spur. Follow it all the way back down to **le Bourget**, where you cross over a bridge. Follow a track through the hamlet back towards the chapel where the walk began.

You are now in Italy.

WALK 15
Lac des Cordes

Start/finish	Le Bourgea (1980m, UTM 32T 326220 4969356)
Distance	10km
Ascent/descent	680m
Grade	Medium
Time	3hr 45min
Maximum altitude	2601m
Map	IGN 3536OT Briançon (1:25,000)
Refreshments	Refuge at les Fonts
Access	From the bottom of the hill below Briançon's old town, follow signs for Col d'Izoard on the D902 towards Cervières. At Cervières, turn left (signposted 'les Fonts'). Follow signs for les Fonts to the hamlet of le Bourgea. Park on the left just before the hamlet or alternatively, turn right just before the hamlet onto a gravel track to a parking area by a bridge

This is not one of the longest routes but the views are among the finest. Besides the tranquil Lac des Cordes, set in a lovely mountain cirque, the walk also crosses a nice col and descends through fine grassy terrain, with fantastic views of the Queyras, another picturesque but relatively unknown region of the Alps. An added advantage is that this remote part of the Briançonnais seems to attract fewer visitors.

The first section of the ascent is quite steep, and a short section makes use of cables to ascend some very steep rock steps. Likewise, a few sections of the descent are relatively steep. Otherwise, the terrain poses few challenges. Navigation is straightforward as the route is on clear paths throughout.

From the car park at the base of the gravel track, cross the bridge and pick up a path climbing to the SW (signposted 'Lac des Cordes'). The steep path winds its way up through a larch forest.

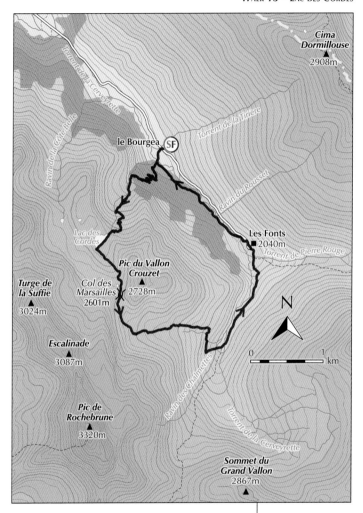

After about 35min, arrive at a very steep rock step which has cables to help you to scramble up it. This section is short and not too challenging but one man's hill

View of the stunning Lac des Cordes from the path to Col des Marsailles

The pink Alpenrose here in summer is something to behold.

is another man's mountain, so take care. Do not take the path which bears around to the right, avoiding the cabled section.

After the cables, continue on the path which now heads into a mountain cirque. As you gain some height, there are super views back down into the Cerveyrette Valley. ◄

Eventually, the path arrives at the magnificent **Lac des Cordes** (2446m, 1hr 15min), surely one of the most spectacular lakes in all of the Alps. You can proceed around either side of the lake but the path on the SE side is more scenic: when you reach the lake keep left and walk the whole way along its SE side to the SW corner. From here, turn left and take a path climbing SE across the grassy slopes.

Follow the path all the way to **Col des Marsailles** (2601m, 2hr). Take a path on the right which initially runs SW and descends the right flank of the valley below. The path makes its way down through grassy terrain – it is steep and rocky in a few places. To the SE you will see the mountains of the Queyras.

When the path arrives at a junction with a signpost (2hr 35min) keep right (signposted 'Col Péas'). After 5min, the path crosses a stream and continues on the other side. After another 5min, arrive at a junction of paths with a signpost: turn left and descend to the E.

After another 5min, arrive at another junction of paths – keep straight ahead (NE) in the direction of a signpost for 'les Fonts'. Shortly afterwards, cross a footbridge over a river and continue on the path heading N on the other side. You now enjoy a descent through a luscious green valley littered with wild flowers in spring.

After a while, the path heads up a small rise and, at the top, the hamlet of les Fonts comes into view at the base of the valley below. Keep on the path until a bridge that leads into **les Fonts** (2040m, 3hr 20min).

The way leads between **ancient buildings** which give you a vivid glimpse of what Alpine life must have been like in days gone by.

The route descends through this lovely valley towards the hamlet of les Fonts

Les Fonts is a good place to stop for refreshments

Walk through the hamlet, then leave the road to turn left down into a parking area. Shortly afterwards turn right on a track heading N (red and white waymarks). After a minute or so, cross the river on a bridge and follow a track running down the left bank of the river all the way back to le Bourgea (3hr 45min).

AYES VALLEY

The plateau of Plan Peyron is the starting point for Walks 17 and 19

WALK 16
Lac du Plan Vallon

Start/finish	The hamlet of le Mélézin (1879m, UTM 32T 313586 4969877)
Distance	6.5km
Ascent/descent	438m
Grade	Easy
Time	2hr 45min
Maximum altitude	2315m
Map	IGN 3536OT Briançon (1:25,000)
Refreshments	None
Access	From the bottom of the hill below Briançon's old town, follow signs for 'Villard-St-Pancrace' and 'Gare SNCF'. Pass the station on your right and follow the road round to the left, signed 'Villard-St-Pancrace'. At Villard-St-Pancrace follow signs for 'Centre Village'. At a junction with a board covered in signs, keep left onto Rue du Mélézin in the direction of 'les Ayes'. Follow signs for 'les Ayes': the road snakes through buildings and then narrows before a junction signposted 'le Mélézin 6.9km'. Turn right onto a forest road leading to le Mélézin: the forest road is not sealed all the way but the gravel surface is generally good and is normally passable by car. Parking is limited in le Mélézin, so park on one of the verges or grassy areas.

This walk starts in a classic alpine hamlet, ascends through pristine larch forest and then emerges onto a wonderful 'balcony' path with magnificent views into the Écrins National Park. It then climbs to a high plateau filled with wild flowers and finally into an exquisite mountain cirque with a lake. Not bad for a walk lasting just under three hours!

The route is not long and poses few difficulties with navigation. However, the short section just before arrival onto the plateau of Plan Vallon is steep and rocky. This route is relatively unused (even by the standards of the Briançonnais) and there is not even a sign indicating the start of the route. Accordingly, you are unlikely to encounter a soul.

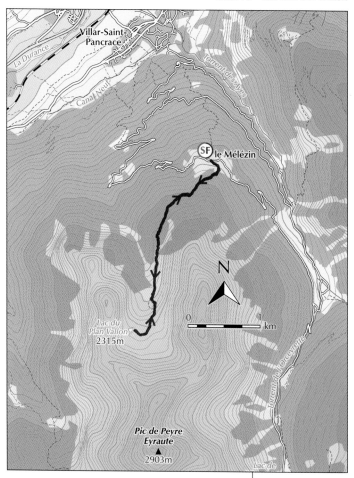

To start, take the track directly opposite the fountain in the centre of le Mélézin, heading uphill to the SE. The track quickly climbs between a number of chalets. The gradient soon levels off before the route begins to climb again less steeply.

The remote hamlet of le Mélézin is a hidden gem

After around 30min arrive at a crossroads of forest tracks and keep ahead (SW). After another 10mins the track narrows to a grassy path. The path now runs alongside an ancient irrigation canal. ▶

Soon the path leaves the trees and the views become more expansive. Here you will catch the first glimpse up ahead of the mountain cirque that you will enter later.

Cross a stream (1hr 5min from the start) and continue on the path. Shortly afterwards, the path splits: keep left. After a few more minutes arrive at a ruined cabin. Here leave the path and head briefly SE across the grassy slope aiming for another path about 100m in front of you to the SE. Continue up this path (S).

Arrive at Plan Vallon (1hr 25min), a grassy plateau leading into the heart of the cirque, and head S across the it. After a few minutes pick up a small path heading up to the SW – follow it to arrive at the **Lac du Plan Vallon** (2315m, 1hr 40min).

> The **Lac du Plan Vallon** is quite shallow and can be a little silted at times – in a hot summer it may even dry up. However, the mountain bowl in which it sits is spectacular and should not be missed. The marmots here are very friendly!

From the lake, simply retrace your steps back to the start (2hr 45m).

Cuckoos are abundant here in spring: you are much more likely to hear them than to see them.

WALK 17
Col des Ayes

Start/finish	Plan Peyron (1870m, UTM 32T 314639 4966972)
Distance	11km
Ascent/descent	612m
Grade	Medium
Time	3hr 30min
Maximum altitude	2477m
Map	IGN 3536OT Briançon (1:25,000)
Refreshments	None
Access	From the bottom of the hill below Briançon's old town, follow signs for 'Villard-St-Pancrace' and 'Gare SNCF'. Pass the station on your right and follow the road round to the left, signposted 'Villard-St-Pancrace'. At Villard-St-Pancrace follow signs for 'Centre Village'. At a junction with a big board covered in signs keep left onto Rue du Mélézin in the direction of 'les Ayes'. Follow the signs for les Ayes: the road initially snakes through buildings and then narrows to arrive at a junction signposted 'le Mélézin 6.9km'. Turn left onto a forest road to Chalets des Ayes: the forest road is not sealed all the way but the gravel surface is generally good and should be passable by car. Drive through Chalets des Ayes, cross a bridge and soon, at a junction, turn left (signposted 'Lac de l'Orceyrette'). Keep on this road until Plan Peyron. There is plenty of parking here.

The walk starts at Plan Peyron, an exceptionally picturesque picnic spot beside a crystal clear river which surrounded on all sides by snowy peaks. The destination, Col des Ayes at 2477m, is a bona fide high alpine col. On the way there, the route passes through forest to enter a grassy pasture with fantastic views down the Ayes Valley.

Much of the climb is on an easy track and only the last section prior to the col is steep. The route is best kept for a fine day as the wind on the exposed col can be fierce.

Take the track which runs uphill from the NE side of the car park. The track ascends gently through pristine larch forest for quite some time. ▶ When the track bears round to head SE you will see, through the trees, the Crête des Granges on your left.

After about 40min on the track, ignore a forest track descending to the left and continue on the main track. The track crosses over the river about 50min from the start and continues climbing on the other side. You can

If you start early in the morning there is a good chance of catching a glimpse of a deer on this track.

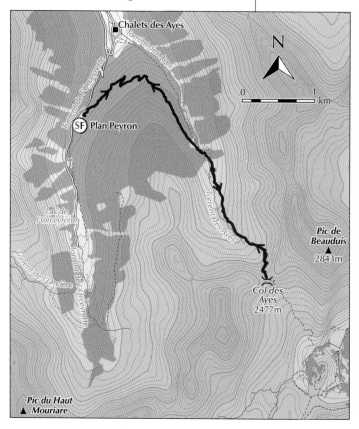

continue up the track but it is more pleasant to take a small path on the right (a few metres after crossing the bridge) which heads uphill to the E. This path meets the track again after about 5min. Meeting the track, turn right and continue uphill.

You are now following the GR5 long distance route. Where the track zigzags back and forth you can save some time by cutting a few corners.

Soon the track climbs among scenic grassy pastures set in a high mountain cirque.

> In the spring the **wild flowers** here are staggering: a carpet of colours stretching endlessly across the grassy slopes.

Approaching a couple of chalets, you will see the Col des Ayes ahead. Shortly after the chalets, where the track bends round to the right, take a faint path heading S alongside a stream towards a signpost just up ahead. The path soon becomes rocky and much better defined and you will be guided by the occasional red and white

The grassy slopes of the Ayes Valley

waymark. Follow the path all the way to the col – the final ascent is quite steep in places.

At the **Col des Ayes** (2477m, 2hr) an entirely new view (of the Queyras) to the S reveals itself.

To descend simply retrace your steps all the way to the car park (3hr 30min).

WALK 18

Fort de la Croix de Bretagne and la Grande Maye

Start/finish	Maison d'Enfants to the NE of Villard-St-Pancrace (1328m, UTM 32T 313725 4972365)
Distance	18.5km
Ascent/descent	1180m
Grade	Very hard
Time	6hr
Maximum altitude	2417m
Map	IGN 3536OT Briançon (1:25,000)
Refreshments	None
Access	From the bottom of the hill below Briançon's old town, follow signs for 'Villard-St-Pancrace' and 'Gare SNCF'. Pass the station on the right and follow the road round to the left, following signs for 'Villard-St-Pancrace'. At Villard-St-Pancrace follow signs for 'Centre Village'. At a junction with a big board covered in signs, keep left onto Rue du Mélézin towards 'les Ayes' and 'Maison d'Enfants'. Follow signs for 'Maison d'Enfants'. At a signpost on the wall of a house, turn left up a road to arrive at the car park beside Maison d'Enfants. Note that there are two Maisons d'Enfants in Villard-St-Pancrace: make sure you head for the one to the NE of the town.

Military history buffs will love this route as it takes in two fantastic old forts. Each of the forts is very different but they both provide magnificent views. The higher of the two, la Grande Maye, offers a complete 360° panorama and each of Briançon's five valleys can be clearly seen. This is also possibly the best viewpoint from which to appreciate Briançon's defences and to understand how each of the forts fitted into the town's defensive strategy. However, even if you have little interest in forts, the views are still exceptional throughout.

This long walk passes over clearly defined paths and tracks, with a section at the end on a gravel road (running down the picturesque Ayes Valley). Navigation is straightforward.

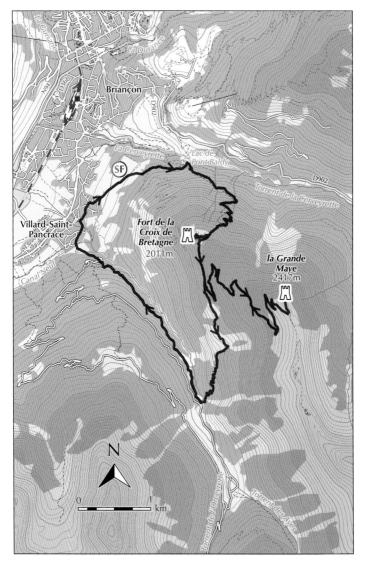

125

From the car park, head back to the road and turn left (NE) on a track signposted 'Fort de la Croix de Bretagne'. After a few minutes, the track arrives at a junction: keep straight ahead, ignoring the tracks to the left and right. About 10min from the car park, at a junction of tracks, keep straight ahead, following another sign for 'Fort de la Croix de Bretagne'.

After 5min, where the path forks, head right on a track heading uphill (signposted 'Fort de la Croix de Bretagne'). ◄

Up to the left you will see the Fort du Randouillet and Fort de l'Infernet.

After a few more minutes the track loops around to the right. In the inside of the loop is a cairn and a path heading up to the right: take this path and, after a few metres, follow a sign for 'Fort de la Croix de Bretagne'. The path climbs steeply through a pine forest.

From Fort de la Croix de Bretagne, the hamlet of le Mélézin can be seen on the other side of the Ayes Valley

After a relentless climb, arrive at **Fort de la Croix de Bretagne** (2011m, 1hr 40min) and head around to the S side of the fort (in a clockwise direction). Arriving at a sign for 'Fort de la Croix de Bretagne (retour)' (coordinates UTM 32T 314875 4971497) head W on a grassy

track. From here, it is well worth taking the time to climb up on top of the fort – access through the seemingly impregnable walls is via a hole in the S side of the fort. To find the hole from the grassy track, follow a faint path off to the right which will lead you along the S side of the fort and past the hole itself. Watch your step as you climb up over the stones to arrive on the roof of the fort. The views from here are spectacular but be careful where you put your feet while on top, as there are many troughs and pits in the grassy surface.

> As technology advanced and the range of artillery increased, it became necessary to construct a series of outlying forts around Briançon to protect against enemy batteries whose canons could now reach the city. **Fort de la Croix de Bretagne** was built between 1874 and 1879 to help counter threats from the Italian border and in particular to protect Briançon against attack from the Cerveyrette Valley. The defences were further strengthened by the construction of a second fort, Fort de l'Infernet, between 1876 and 1878 on the other side of the Cerveyrette Valley.
>
> Fort de la Croix de Bretagne was constructed on a number of levels on the slope of a rocky outcrop. It had a garrison of 500 men, 16 guns and two magazines (of 47 and 75 tons respectively).

Descend back to the grassy track and turn right (W). After a few minutes on the track, descend to the left (S) to meet a gravel track: turn left and head S along it. ▶

Note that if you turn right instead, the track will take you on a worthwhile detour to the front of the fort.

After 10min on this track, at a fork, take the left fork to climb on a stony track. The climb on the track is long and a little wearisome, but the views through the trees are excellent throughout and the panorama at the top is well worth the effort.

After about 15min on the stony track, at a left-hand hairpin, ignore a grassy track heading S and continue up the main track. Eventually, the track passes just below the S side of the fort of la Grande Maye and, shortly

La Grande Maye has a commanding position above Briançon

afterwards, arrives at an old stone bunker (on the left) with metal doors. Leave the track before the bunker and climb the grassy slope to the NE until you meet the track again. Turn left along the track and climb to **la Grande Maye** (2417m, 3hr 15min).

> Rest here and savour the 360° panoramas – most of the other forts of the Briançonnais are visible from here. **La Grande Maye**, a small fort built between 1886 and 1888, was used as an observation post for neighbouring batteries. The fort garrisoned 50–80 infantry soldiers and also protected Briançon from enemy infantry assault from Italy or across the Col d'Izoard.

From the fort, retrace your steps back down the track. For a shortcut, after a few minutes from the fort, at a cairn on your right, take a small path heading W and follow it down to meet the track again.

Continue all the way down the track to arrive back at the junction of tracks which you passed earlier (4hr 10min). Turn left to descend to the S. After 5min the path emerges from the trees onto a grassy plateau with superb views. Keep following this path as it makes its way down into the Ayes Valley to arrive at the **Torrent des Ayes** (4hr 50min). Cross a footbridge over the torrent and climb briefly up a path on the other side to arrive at a gravel road (D236T). Turn right and walk NW down the gravel road.

After about 40min on the road, arrive at a signpost on the right (1390m) – leave the road here in favour of a path (signposted 'Fort de la Croix de Bretagne (retour)'). Shortly afterwards, reaching a road, cross over and descend the short ravine on the other side. Arrive at the road again and descend on it.

Shortly after the Chapelle St Laurent, where the road bends sharply to the left, leave the road in favour of a smaller road heading N (red and white waymark). After a few minutes, at a tree with red and white way-marks on it, leave the road in favour of a path on the left. When the path arrives at another road, turn right and head NE. The road squeezes between buildings: just afterwards, at a junction, turn right in the direction of a sign for 'Maison d'Enfants' – this is the road you drove along earlier. Head along the road to arrive back at the car park on the left (6hr).

Briançon and the Guisane Valley as seen from Fort de la Croix de Bretagne

WALK 19

Lac de l'Orceyrette

Start/finish	Plan Peyron (1870m, UTM 32T 314639 4966972)
Distance	8.5km
Ascent/descent	355m
Grade	Easy
Time	3hr
Maximum altitude	2183m
Map	IGN 3536 OT Briançon (1:25,000)
Refreshments	None
Access	From the bottom of the hill below Briançon's old town, follow signs for 'Villard-St-Pancrace' and 'Gare SNCF'. Pass the station on your right and follow the road round to the left, following signs for 'Villard-St-Pancrace'. At Villard-St-Pancrace follow signs for 'Centre Village'. At a junction with a big board covered in signs, keep left onto Rue du Mélézin towards 'les Ayes'. Keep following signs for les Ayes as the road snakes through buildings then narrows, reaching a junction with a signpost for 'le Mélézin 6.9km'. Turn left here and follow a forest road to Chalets des Ayes – the forest road is not sealed all the way but the gravel surface is generally good and is normally passable by car. Drive through Chalets des Ayes, cross a bridge and shortly afterwards turn left at a junction (signposted 'Lac de l'Orceyrette'). Keep on this road until Plan Peyron. There is plenty of parking here.

This stunning little walk is perfect for all ages, particularly on a hot day because most of the climb is in a shady larch forest. Visiting an exceptionally serene part of the Ayes Valley, the highlight of the route is the pretty and peaceful alpine meadow of the Chalets de la Taure. A delightful walk follows along a 'balcony' path with fantastic views. Then the path descends into the valley to one of the prettiest lakes in the whole of the region.

The whole route is on clear paths and tracks and navigation is straightforward.

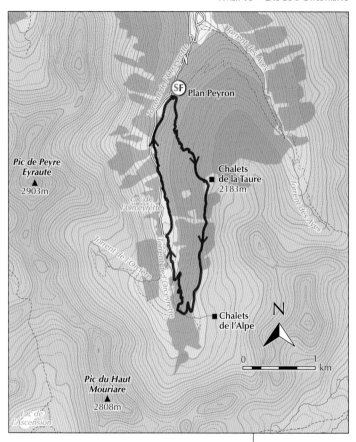

The walk starts at Plan Peyron, an exceptionally picturesque picnic spot beside a crystal clear river surrounded
on all sides by snowy peaks. Take the track which runs
uphill from the NE side of the car park. After a couple
of minutes, turn right at a rock (with a faint arrow on it)
to climb on a path to the S. The path zigzags back and
forwards as it ascends through a larch forest.

View from Chalets de la Taure

This is a beautiful place for a picnic.

At a junction of paths (45–50min), keep left on the main path – the right-hand branch descends back to Plan Peyron which would be a frustrating mistake to make! As you approach the chalets 5–10min later, arrive at a little junction: keep straight ahead to arrive at **Chalets de la Taure** (2183m, 1hr). ◄

From the southernmost chalet, pick up a small path heading S. After a few minutes, arrive at a junction of paths and keep straight ahead towards the S. As the path undulates, not gaining or losing much height, the views to the E are fantastic.

Arrive at a pasture filled with wild flowers (1hr 30min). There is a junction of paths here which can be hard to spot in early summer if the grass is very long. If you are feeling energetic, you could take the left fork and vary the route by making the short climb up to the **Chalets de l'Alpe** and then rejoining the main route on your descent.

Otherwise, to continue on the recommended route, take the right fork and keep on the main path to the S.

When the path arrives at a track (1hr 50min), turn right and descend on it.

After 5mins on the track, at a junction of tracks, keep right. At another junction of tracks, keep straight ahead towards the Lac de l'Orceyrette, which you will now see up ahead. Eventually, the path the track bends around to the left towards a footbridge over the **Torrent de l'Orceyrette**. Do not cross the bridge – instead, immediately after the left-hand bend, take a small path heading N towards the lake.

When the path arrives at a barrier, keep straight ahead along the track towards the lake. Shortly afterwards, leave this track in favour of another track on the right – follow this in the direction of a chalet. Then after a few more minutes, leave the track in favour of a path on the left (signposted 'Sentier'). After a few more minutes, arrive at the E side of **Lac de l'Orceyrette** (1927m, 2hr 30min).

Follow the path all the way along the E side of the lake. From the N tip of the lake, keep ahead on the path which runs down the right bank of the Torrent de

The gorgeous Lac de l'Orceyrette

This stunning route can be enjoyed by all the family

l'Orceyrette. Where the path forks, you can take either fork as both meet up after a few minutes. Keep N on the path to arrive back at **Plan Peyron** (3hr).

DURANCE VALLEY

Early morning reflections of the Tête des Lauzières (Walk 28)

WALK 20
Lac Palluel and Lac Faravel

Start/finish	Car park below Dormillouse (1440m, UTM 32T 298101 4956516)
Distance	14km
Ascent/descent	1080m
Grade	Hard
Time	5hr 10min
Maximum altitude	2479m
Map	IGN 3437ET Orcières-Merlette (1:25,000)
Refreshments	None
Access	Take the N94 S from Briançon for about 20km. After l'Argentière-la-Bessée take the exit on the right (signposted 'Freissinières'). Follow the D38 to Freissinières. Then head W on the D238 until the road runs out at a car park. Park on the S side of the car park and not on the river side – the river erodes the bank on the N side and cars have been washed into the river.

This walk in the Écrins National Park is absolutely magnificent. It takes in two exquisite high altitude lakes, each of them set in a different, yet equally glorious, mountain bowl. On a calm day, the reflection of the mountains in the glassy waters of the lakes is out of this world. The pink Alpenrose also features here in June and July. This is a Briançonnais classic.

Most of the route is on clear paths. However, the final climb to Lac Palluel is across steep rocky slopes. Also, care should be taken in low visibility as it would be easy to get disorientated – the lake itself does not show itself until the last moment so there is nothing to aim for except the many cairns which have been strategically placed. Needless to say, this route is best saved for a fine day. Also be aware that snow can lie at the lakes until the end of June. The author can confirm that navigation to, and between, the lakes is quite difficult in the snow!

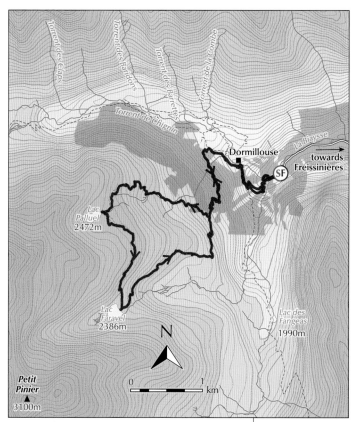

From the SW side of the car park take the path signed towards 'Dormillouse'. Almost immediately, cross a footbridge and begin to ascend. As the climb progresses, the waterfall on the right dominates your attention. ▶

At a signpost, turn right towards Dormillouse and continue to climb. At the next signpost keep heading uphill to the right.

As the snow melts in spring and early summer the volume of water coming over the waterfall is staggering.

Dormillouse and the Freissinières Valley as seen from the path to Lac Palluel

As the path rises there are **stunning views** of the Freissinières Valley and as you get closer to the gorge to the N the sound of the waterfall is exhilarating.

At the next fork keep right in the direction of a small arrow on a post. Shortly afterwards, at another junction, keep right. After a few more minutes you reach yet another junction: this time turn left (signed towards 'Lac Faravel' and 'Lac Palluel').

At another sign for 'Lac Palluel' and 'Lac Faravel', 30mins from the start, turn left onto a small path. As you ascend you will see the hamlet of **Dormillouse** on your right.

After another 5–10min, at a signpost, keep left along the main path (signed to 'Lac Palluel' and 'Lac Faravel'). After another five minutes, turn left at another signpost and ignore the signpost to 'Dormillouse par les Romans'.

Shortly afterwards, the path passes over a waterfall on a footbridge, from where there are views of Dormillouse. Keep climbing and eventually the path emerges from the trees (1hr 15min), giving spectacular views. Shortly afterwards, arrive at another signpost and turn right in the direction of Lac Palluel. ▶

In summer much of the hillside is covered with vibrant pink Alpenrose.

After about 15min the path becomes faint as it crosses a rocky step –there is a cairn to guide you. Soon afterwards, the path fords a stream and continues uphill on the other side. You really do feel like you are in the high mountains now. After another 10min the path fords a couple more streams and then climbs a rocky slope – again watch out for cairns to guide you.

About 2hr from the start, climb over some large rocky steps with a cairn on top: be careful in the wet as this can be slippery. Shortly afterwards, continue up over some more rocks (with guiding cairns) to arrive onto a rocky plateau (2hr 5min). Continue climbing to the W, again following cairns.

After a few minutes, arrive on a clear path again. When the path disappears once more, keep on the look-out for more cairns as you head up the hillside to the SW. In low visibility it would be easy to get disorientated here. Arrive at **Lac Palluel** (2472m, 2hr 25min), set in a huge mountain cirque.

From the lake head E on a rocky path which soon bears round to the SE as it descends briefly towards a plateau with hundreds of small cairns built on it. Head through the cairn 'field' and out the other side in a SE direction to arrive on a clear path again. Follow this path as it contours around the side of the hill to the SE and then S. About 30min from Lac Palluel you will catch your first glimpse of Lac Faravel below, set on a mountain plateau.

The path descends to arrive at **Lac Faravel** (2386m, 3hr 10min).

Although the lake lies in the Écrins National Park, **camping** is permitted here for one night and it makes a magnificent place to bivouac.

Snow can remain at Lac Faravel until late June

From the lake, head E in the direction of a large cairn on a rock. Here you will pick up a path which descends to the NE. After a few minutes the path becomes hard to discern as it descends a rocky slope. Pick up the path again at the bottom of the rocks and continue along it as it contours across the side of a wide valley.

Eventually, the path starts to descend again and when the path splits (4hr) keep left towards the S. After a few more minutes, at a signpost, where the path splits again, head downhill towards the E.

Shortly afterwards, follow the path as it bears around to the N to reach the junction and signpost you passed earlier (4hr 15min). Keep straight ahead towards Dormillouse and retrace your steps back to the car park (5hr 10min).

WALK 21

Lac de Fangeas

Start/finish	Car park below Dormillouse (1440m, UTM 32T 298101 4956516)
Distance	7km
Ascent/descent	550m
Grade	Medium
Time	2hr 40min
Maximum altitude	1990m
Map	IGN 3437ET Orcières-Merlette (1:25,000)
Refreshments	None
Access	Take the N94 S from Briançon for about 20km. After the town of l'Argentière-la-Bessée, exit right (signposted 'Freissinières'). Follow the D38 to Freissinières. Then head W on the D238 until the road runs out at a car park. Park on the S side of the car park and not on the river side – the river erodes the bank on the N side and cars have been washed into the river

This is a stunning short walk to a magnificent high alpine lake, set in a lovely hanging valley and surrounded by snow-capped peaks. In autumn the colours of the trees are a sight to behold. The walk is on clear paths and navigation is straightforward.

The walk may be extended by a visit to the hamlet of Dormillouse.

From the SW side of the car park take the path signed towards 'Dormillouse'. Almost immediately, cross a footbridge and begin to ascend.

As the climb progresses, the **waterfall** on the right dominates your attention. As the snow melts in spring, the volume of water coming down the waterfall is staggering.

To the E are glorious
views down into
the valley.

At a signpost, 25min from the car park, turn left towards 'Lac de Fangeas' and continue to climb. ◄ After 5–10min the path ascends a series of rocks which can be slippery after rainfall.

At the next signpost, keep straight ahead on the main track to the S. The path continues to climb through the trees, and 1hr 5min from the start crosses a wooden footbridge across a torrent. The path emerges above the tree line, 1hr 25min from the start, and climbs a rock step – look out for a cairn on top of the rocks.

Keep climbing alongside the river for a few more minutes to reach **Lac de Fangeas** (1990m, 1hr 30min). On a fine day this is a wonderful place for a picnic.

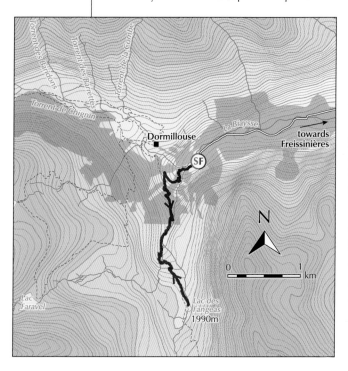

From the lake simply retrace your steps all the way back down to the car park.

A walker descending from Lac Fangeas

If you wish to extend your walk, then 40mins after leaving the lake, take a left turn at a signpost. From here, it is about 30min to the hamlet of **Dormillouse**. This path is mostly through trees and is a bit rougher than the main path. From Dormillouse, simply follow the signs back down to the car park.

WALK 22
Dormillouse High Circuit

Start/finish	Car park below Dormillouse (1440m, UTM 32T 298101 4956516)
Distance	7.75km
Ascent/descent	580m
Grade	Medium
Time	2hr 45min
Maximum altitude	1850m
Map	IGN 3437ET Orcières-Merlette (1:25,000)
Refreshments	There may be refreshments available in Dormillouse in summer
Access	Take the N94 S from Briançon for about 20km. After l'Argentière-la-Bessée, exit right (signposted 'Freissinières'). Follow the D38 to Freissinières. Head W on the D238 until the road runs out at a car park. Park on the S side of the car park and not on the river side – the river erodes the bank on the N side and cars have been washed into the river.

This is a short but rewarding walk into the stunning Chichin Valley, flanked by jagged peaks. Numerous waterfalls cascade over the cliffs into the valley and this is a spectacular setting for a picnic. The route also visits the ancient buildings of the hamlet of Dormillouse.

This walk would normally be graded 'easy'. However, at the time of writing, floods had damaged a footbridge, silted up some paths and eroded the walls of a gully. These issues make the walk slightly more challenging and, accordingly, it has been graded 'medium'.

From the SW side of the car park take the path signed towards 'Dormillouse'. Almost immediately, cross a footbridge and begin to ascend.

As the climb progresses, the **waterfall** on the right dominates your attention. As the snow melts in spring and early summer, the volume of water coming down the waterfall is staggering.

At a signpost 25min from the car park, turn right towards 'Dormillouse' and continue to climb. At the next signpost keep heading uphill to the right.

As the path rises there are **stunning views** of the Freissinières Valley and as you get closer to the gorge to the N the sound of the waterfall is exhilarating.

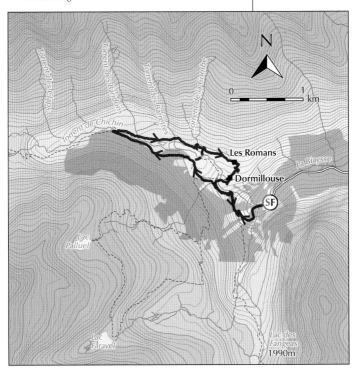

The beautiful Chichin Valley

The rugged Crête de Dormillouse looms large in front of you and many waterfalls tumble down the high cliff faces.

At the next fork keep right in the direction of a small arrow on a post. Shortly afterwards, at another junction, keep right. After a few more minutes you reach yet another junction – this time turn left (signed towards 'Lac Faravel' and 'Lac Palluel'). As you ascend, you will see **Dormillouse** on your right.

After 5–10min leave the main path at a signpost and head to the right to climb on a faint path in the direction of 'Col de Freissinières'. After 5min the terrain opens out into the grasslands of the Chichin Valley. ◀

At a signpost turn left towards 'Col de Freissinières'. The path heads back into the trees and levels off. After a few minutes the path emerges from trees and bends towards the river. From here, the view of the waterfalls is magnificent.

The path arrives just above the river 1hr 25min into the walk. Turn right onto another path which rises up to meet the path you are on – be careful, this path would be easy to miss. Follow the path a short distance to the NE until it meets the **Torrent de Chichin** and a footbridge. Cross the bridge.

At the time of writing, the bridge had been partly damaged by floods but was passable with care. If the bridge does not look safe then head back the way you came and return to the signpost for 'Col de Freissinières'. Then turn left (signposted 'Dormillouse par les Romans') and follow the path to les Romans. From there, follow the instructions below – it is not worth taking any risks and it is hardly an imposition to have to return through such beautiful scenery!

Turn right immediately after the bridge and head back downstream. At the time of writing, parts of the path had become covered with silt from a flood and were not discernible. However, you should not go wrong if you stick close to the river for 5– 10min: you will be heading roughly E. Occasionally there are cairns to indicate the route.

Soon the path disappears completely as you cross a boulder field. Pick up the path again on the far side and head towards a cairn in front of you. Shortly after the cairn, the path becomes obvious again.

The chapel in Dormillouse

Be very careful here as the gully walls have been recently eroded by a flood and are fairly steep.

Cross over another small stream and pick up the path again on the far side. Now the path moves away from the river for a while and eventually it loops round to the left to arrive at a large gully. ◄ Pick your way down the side of the gully and then there will be a short scramble up the other side.

On the other side of the gully, head for a path which you can see in front of you to the left. Go E on this path to reach **les Romans**, a hamlet above Dormillouse. Pass an old millstone on your right and keep along the path between the buildings. Soon the path begins to descend.

At a junction turn left. Pass the buildings of **Dormillouse**, including the old school house. Keep following the main path at a signpost. Eventually the path descends to a bridge: cross this and turn left on the other side. This path crosses a few more footbridges and then brings you onto the path you arrived on earlier. Follow this path back down to the car park (2hr 45min).

WALK 23
Crête de la Rortie

Start/finish	Les Roberts (1413m, UTM 32T 304641 4959157)
Distance	10.25km
Ascent/descent	660m
Grade	Medium
Time	3hr 20min
Maximum altitude	1763m
Map	IGN 3437ET Orcières-Merlette (1:25,000)
Refreshments	None
Access	Take the N94 S from Briançon for about 20km. After l'Argentière-la-Bessée, exit right (signposted 'Freissinières'). Follow the D38 to the entrance to the village of Freissinières. Then turn right onto the D238, following a sign for 'via ferrata'. Climb the narrow road and, at a school, turn right, still following 'via ferrata'. Keep on this road to les Roberts. Park at one of the lay-bys before or in the village. In high season parking may be difficult, so arrive early.

This is a super introduction to the pretty Freissinières Valley and makes for a great outing on a hot day, as part of the walk is through lovely shady trees which regularly open up, giving fantastic views. The route also ascends the narrow Crête de la Rortie with exciting exposure and fantastic views. Towards the middle of the walk, there are some steep and challenging rocky sections on which you must take care. As the altitude is relatively low, this is also a good walk in the spring. Navigation is straightforward. The route could also be undertaken using a via ferrata, for those with the correct experience and equipment (see 'Via ferrata' in the Introduction). Do not attempt the via ferrata without the appropriate equipment and experience.

From les Roberts, follow a sign to 'les Aujards' and take a path heading NW. When the path arrives at the gravel road, turn right onto the road. Shortly afterwards, at a

Via ferrata variation: For this option, park about 0.5km before les Roberts at the corner of a hairpin bend (UTM 32T 305162 4958980). There is a board here indicating the start of the via ferrata. Head initially SE on a path. When you reach a sign for 'via ferrata' take the path on the left and head uphill. At a junction with a signpost turn right to commence the route. After the via ferrata you join the walk route at a junction (see below); from there, simply follow the remainder of the walk.

hairpin, leave the road in favour of a small path heading uphill (there is a red and white waymark on a rock). Arrive at the road again four more times in succession

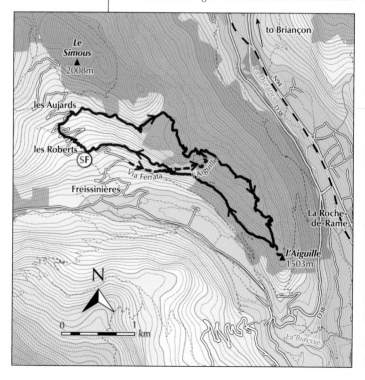

The Durance Valley and the Queyras as seen from Crête de la Rortie

– each time continue up the hillside on the other side on a path.

Cross over a little footbridge and just on the left you will notice some old millstones. Shortly afterwards, arrive at the pretty little hamlet of **les Aujards** (1600m, 30min). Proceed straight ahead on a path through the buildings. In amongst the buildings, arrive at a signpost and turn left towards 'Clot du Puy'. The path levels out 15–20min from les Aujards.

After a while the path begins to climb again and makes its way up through some trees. At a signpost (1hr 5min) keep straight ahead towards 'Clot du Puy'. Keep following the path until it descends to a junction of paths, then turn left and keep descending. Shortly afterwards, arrive at a signpost: the end of the via ferrata also arrives at this junction. Keep straight ahead in the direction of a sign to Col de l'Aiguillette. The path now climbs up the Crête de la Rortie. ▶

As you proceed, the ridge gets narrower and there are great views on both sides.

Eventually, arrive at two trees with green and white marks on them and a green and red sign pointing to the left. This junction is easy to miss so take care. If you go straight ahead here, after a few seconds you'll reach an amazing lookout. To continue on the walk, however, turn left and descend. This is the start of a series of steep and quite challenging sections through some amazing rock formations. The views are superb but watch your step as the path is sometimes very close to the edge of the cliffs. There are a couple of places where you will need to stoop to pass under some low rock arches.

About 2hr 30min from the start, arrive at a signpost.

If you wish to extend the walk then head uphill to the left to **Col de l'Aiguille**, which is an extremely worthwhile side trip (30min there and back to the junction).

To continue on the main route, head downhill towards 'les Roberts'. Soon the path bends around to the NW.

At a junction of paths, turn right in the direction of les Roberts. Shortly afterwards, arrive at a fork and keep right. After 5–10min arrive at another fork, and again keep right.

Soon you pass the starting point for the via ferrata on your right. If you did the via ferrata then keep straight ahead and follow the path back to your car. Otherwise, turn right uphill following the sign for 'via ferrata'. After a few minutes, arrive at a junction with a signpost and follow the sign to 'les Roberts' (NW). The other path going uphill to the right would bring you to the start of the via ferrata.

With les Roberts in sight, keep right at a fork. The path rises briefly and then arrives at another signpost: head left, following the sign to 'les Roberts'. When you reach a vehicle track turn left and head briefly downhill. The track bends round to the right and meets the road. Turn right up the road to arrive back at your car.

WALK 24

La Grande Cabane

Start/finish	Réserve Biologique des Deslioures in the Fournel Valley (1570m, UTM 32T 299069 4962563)
Distance	15km
Ascent/descent	790m
Grade	Hard
Time	5hr
Maximum altitude	2254m
Map	IGN 3437ET Orcières-Merlette (1:25,000)
Refreshments	None
Access	Take the N94 S from Briançon for about 20km. At l'Argentière-la-Bessée turn right into the town centre (signposted 'Vallouise' and 'Puy St Vincent'). At traffic lights in the town centre, turn left (signposted 'Vallé du Fournel'). After 1km go under a railway bridge to a roundabout with an old mining trolley in the centre. Head straight across the roundabout (signposted 'Vallé du Fournel'). After 7.5km the road becomes a gravel road (which is normally passable by all cars). At a junction keep straight ahead in the direction of 'la Salce'. After another 4km arrive at a grassy parking area where the track ends.

This route is spectacular and is one of the author's favourites, set in the unspoilt and little known Fournel Valley. Almost the entire walk is spent on a high balcony running along the N slope of the valley, offering incredible views of snowy peaks and too many waterfalls to count. The walk is above the tree line for almost its entire length. Spring is a particularly lovely time to undertake this route, as the peaks on either side of the valley will still be thick with snow and the wild flowers are staggering. The reserve beside the parking area is a good place to find the rare Chardon Bleu.

The walk follows a path up the valley to the W and then the same path back down again. The gradient is rarely very steep. There are a few places where the path becomes faint as it proceeds through long grass, but if you

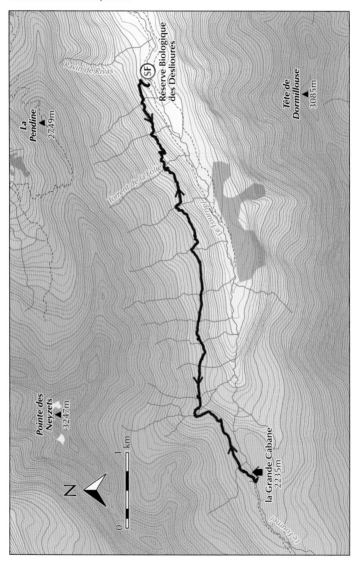

pay attention it is easy to follow – there are waymarks and a few cairns to guide you. There are a number of stream crossings to undertake: these are mostly straightforward but be careful in the spring, when the volume of water is greater. Note that where the route description indicates streams or waterfalls, these can from time to time be dry, depending on the season.

From the car park head NW towards a yellow signpost a few metres away. From the signpost head N on a path (signposted 'la Grande Cabane') which immediately crosses a ravine and continues on the other side. After a few minutes, the path bears around to the W and this will be your general direction all the way to la Grande Cabane – ignore any offshoots branching off the path and keep on the main route.

After about 5min, cross another ravine and continue on the other side. Cross a stream underneath a waterfall about 15min from the start. ▶

About 1hr from the start, the path skirts very close to the edge of steep cliffs – the path is a little unstable in places so watch your footing as a fall could have serious

As you climb, you feel like you could reach out and touch the steep snowy peaks on the other side of the valley.

Carpet of flowers in the Fournel Valley in the spring

The lovely Fournel Valley

consequences. Shortly afterwards, the path descends into a ravine and crosses a stream (1hr 15min). Just after the stream, ignore a path to the left and continue to the right – a red and white cross indicates that the left fork is incorrect.

Soon the path becomes faint as it heads up to the NW – keep on the lookout for red and white waymarks and a cairn on a rock. Shortly after the cairn, follow the path towards the SW through a boulder field and then cross a small stream to arrive back at a clear path. Just after this stream, you will see Cabane de la Balme below you. ◄

The wild flowers here are amazing in spring.

Keep on the main path which now heads across grassy slopes. The grass can be very long, concealing the path. The path does not gain much height for a while until, a few minutes after crossing a ravine (2hr), it starts climbing quite steeply. There now seems to be waterfalls on all sides.

Descend into another ravine (2hr 15min) and cross a stream – be careful here in spring because, as the snow is melting, huge volumes of water pass through making crossing it more difficult. The path now climbs over the top of a grassy spur and continues on the other side. Soon you will be able to see la Grande Cabane up ahead to the SW.

As you approach the cabane, the path heads across a grassy plateau, crosses a few streams and then makes a sharp left turn (indicated by a red and white waymark on a rock) to descend towards the cabane. Arrive at the river directly in front of the cabane and then cross a footbridge to reach the **la Grande Cabane** (2235m, 2hr 45min). ▸

The cabin itself is a little ramshackle but its surroundings are exquisite.

From the cabin simply retrace your steps back to your car. As you descend through the grassy slopes just before Cabane de la Balme do not head down to the cabane itself but aim for a cairn on a rock slightly further up the hillside. The cairn will guide you onto the path you arrived on.

Also, after the boulder field you passed earlier, remember that the path is very faint where it crosses the grassy slopes so be sure to pay attention – there are a few cairns and waymarks. Arrive back at the car park 5hr from the start.

La Grande Cabane has an isolated position high up in the Fournel Valley

157

WALK 25
La Blanche

Start/finish	Foot of the ski lift above Puy Aillaud (1600m, UTM 32T 300900 4970040)
Distance	12km
Ascent/descent	1400m
Grade	Very hard
Time	6hr
Maximum altitude	2953m
Map	IGN 3436ET Meije Pelvoux (1:25,000)
Refreshments	None
Access	Take the N94 S from Briançon for about 20km. At l'Argentière-la-Bessée, turn right (signposted 'Vallouise' and 'Puy-St-Vincent'). At traffic lights in the town centre turn right onto the D994E (signposted 'Vallouise' and 'Puy-St-Vincent') and drive to Vallouise. Turn left to cross the bridge into the village centre and, at a little roundabout in front of the church, turn right (signposted 'Puy Aillaud'). 2km after Vallouise turn right onto the D504. After 4km, at Puy Aillaud, keep on the main road to skirt around the village. Just above the village, arrive at the bottom of a ski lift and a wooden toilet block on the right. Park on the verge here.

La Blanche (2953m) offers one of the finest viewpoints in the whole of the Briançonnais. The summit is just a stone's throw from the Écrins National Park and a number of stunning valleys can be seen below, including the Clapouse and Sélé Valleys. There is also the pretty Lac de Puy Aillaud, which is visited with little effort on the descent. On a fine day, this will be a highlight of a trip to this amazing region.

The altitude gain on this route is great so start early to avoid climbing during the hottest part of the day. The final ascent to the summit is very steep, so watch your footing. Navigation is straightforward, except for the last hour or so before the summit, when you will need to follow cairns over rocky ground. It would be easy to lose your way here in low visibility so do not attempt this route unless the weather is fine.

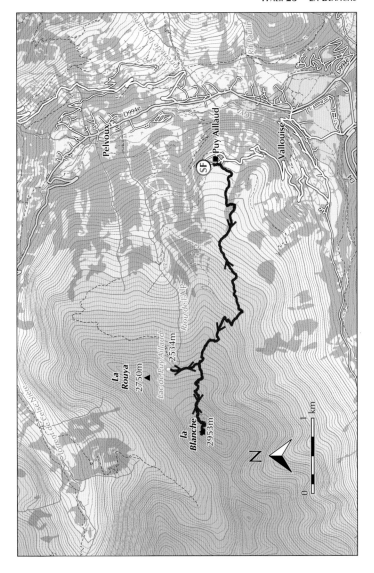

Head S down the road (do not take the track to the NW, signposted 'Belvedere de 3 Refuges'). After a minute, take a track on the right (SW) in the direction of a signpost to 'la Blanche': note that the signpost is slightly concealed and easily missed.

After a few more minutes, take a small path on the right (signposted 'la Blanche') which climbs up the right-hand side of a small valley. The path enters a forest 20min from the start and climbs through it. ◄ The path now climbs to the W on the other side of the small valley. Where the path becomes faint, crossing short grassy sections, keep heading W.

As the path emerges again from the trees, the views into the Vallouise Valley are lovely.

At a junction with a signpost (45min) turn left towards 'la Blanche' to climb on a clear path. The path crosses rocks (with cairns) 10min from the junction and continues on the other side.

After 1hr 50min the path splits: you can take either branch as they will both arrive at the same place eventually, but if in doubt keep following the cairns by taking the left fork. If you have taken the left fork then, shortly afterwards, where the path disappears, head right behind a rock with a cairn on it and after a few metres pick up the path again.

Eventually, the path arrives at a signpost (coordinates UTM 32T 298196 4970335; 2hr 15min). Rather confusingly, the signpost indicates that la Blanche is to the left (S) but this is incorrect: head W straight up the hillside on a faint path towards a cairn. Now follow a series of cairns up the rocky slope, broadly to the W – sometimes the path is clear and sometimes it is not. Generally, where the path is hard to follow there are cairns for guidance: pay attention so that you do not lose them.

Eventually, the path reaches a mountain bowl with la Blanche directly ahead. Now follow the cairns to the SW to climb up the steep rocky slopes, heading broadly towards a little saddle. ◄

Note that snow lies here until late June or early July which can make the final ascent difficult or even impossible.

From the saddle, head NW and climb up to the summit of **la Blanche** (2953m, 3hr 15min).

This is an **excellent spot for a long break** if weather permits. The 360° views into the Vallouise Valley and the Écrins National Park are truly remarkable.

The view towards the Onde valley from the slopes of la Blanche

Once you have managed to drag yourself away from the summit, retrace your steps down to the E and then SE to reach the saddle again. From there, simply retrace your steps back to the signpost. On the descent it is easy to lose the path and the cairns – if you do, then keep heading E and you should pick them up again.

Arrive back at the junction with the signpost (4hr 5min). To visit Lac de Puy Aillaud from here, head N (signposted 'Lac de Puy Aillaud'). After a few minutes, you will see the lake up ahead and pick up a faint path.

The **views into the Vallouise Valley** are amazing and the dome shaped summit of la Condamine can clearly be seen across the valley.

Soon the path becomes faint and rocky so watch your footing. Arrive at **Lac de Puy Aillaud** (2534m, 4hr 15min).

From the lake, simply retrace your steps back to the signpost, turn left and retrace your steps to the start (6hr).

WALK 26

Chapelle St Hippolyte

Start/finish	D4 near Prelles (1240m, UTM 32T 308488 4968072)
Distance	4km
Ascent/descent	270m
Grade	Easy
Time	1hr 30min
Maximum altitude	1501m
Map	IGN 3536OT Briançon (1:25,000)
Refreshments	None
Access	From Briançon head SW on the N94 for about 7km. At Prelles turn right on the D4 towards 'les Vigneaux'. After 1.5km park at a grassy parking area on the right.
Note	The chapel is closed to the public but the key can be requested at the Gîte du Pas du Loup in Bouchier, a short walk from the chapel.

This is a super little walk to what must be one of the most beautiful and remote chapels in all of the Alps. The relatively low altitude means that the route can be tackled even in the spring.

From the car park, head N up a track. After a few minutes, at a signpost on your left, turn left, following the sign to 'Chapelle St Hippolyte'. Keep on this main path and do not leave it for any off-shoots – regular red and white waymarks indicate that you are on the correct path.

After 15–20min keep on the main path, ignoring another path which heads W uphill at a cairn. Reach a post (in a clearing), with a red and white waymark on it, 30–40min from the start, from where the chapel can be seen up on the left. Turn left at the post and follow a faint path in the direction of the chapel.

Aim for the right-hand side of the rocky hill on which the chapel rests: here you will find the path for the final

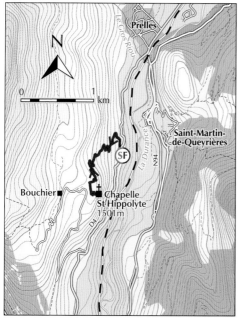

Chapelle St. Hippolyte is one of finest of the region's many mountain chapels

The hamlet of Bouchier can be seen from the chapel

ascent to the chapel itself. Follow this path upwards, sometimes quite steeply. The path climbs over rocks and skirts the edge of the hill in places, so watch your step. After 5min on the path, arrive at the **Chapelle St Hippolyte** (1501m, 50min).

> The **Chapel St Hippolyte** dates from 1509 and has beautiful murals inside. It attracted the sick who hoped for a cure from Saint Hippolytus.

To descend, retrace your steps back down the chapel's rocky hill. At the bottom of the hill, head N to pick up a small path ahead and follow this to arrive at the post with the red and white waymark again. Turn right and retrace your steps to the start (1hr 30min).

WALK 27

Croix de la Salcette

Start/finish	Bouchier (1745m, UTM 32T 307971 4967510)
Distance	10.5km
Ascent/descent	870m
Grade	Hard
Time	4hr
Maximum altitude	2331m
Map	IGN 3536OT Briançon (1:25,000)
Refreshments	None
Access	Take the N94 SW from Briançon. Just after Prelles, take the D4 towards 'les Vigneaux' and after 3km take a gravel track on the right towards 'Bouchier'. After about 3km, park at a grassy parking area on the right with a signpost for 'Chapelle St Hippolyte'.

This little used route passes through a magnificent cirque hidden from the outside world. It then climbs up to a beautiful mountain plateau with expansive views on all sides and where the elusive Edelweiss can often be found. Finally it passes through the old stone buildings of the remote hamlet of Bouchier.

Although the descent from Croix de la Salcette is a real knee-jerker, being extremely steep in places with a couple of sections that call for some scrambling, it is worth it for the views. Route finding is a little tricky at times.

Walk up the road towards Bouchier for about 5min. Ignore the first track you see on your right. When you come to a fork, take the right branch. Almost immediately afterwards, at a signpost, turn right on a track heading uphill (to the N).

1hr from the start, at a right-hand bend, there is a faint path on the left (heading upwards to the NW). Be careful as this junction (coordinates UTM 32T 307138 4970330) would be very easy to miss. At the junction there is a stream running into the apex of the bend in the track and there is a small marker on a tree indicating 'no.10'.

Climb up this steep little path, initially alongside the **Torrent de Combe Brune**. Soon emerge from the trees

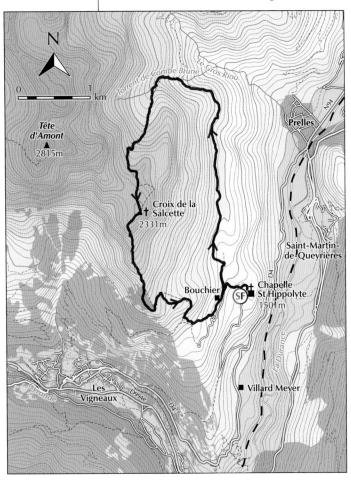

into a rocky ravine. The path bears left and heads W up the ravine into a huge mountain cirque that you would never know existed. In front is the massif of Mont Brison. Ignore any paths branching off from the main path: these are used by climbers to access the steep rock faces.

The hidden cirque in the shadow of Mont Brison

Where the path leaves the trees and enters a huge boulder field, turn left at a junction and follow the path across a rocky slope – cairns assist with navigation. After the rocky slope, keep ahead following the path uphill to the SE. Where the path is faint, follow the cairns.

Soon you will arrive on top of a broad plateau (2hr 10min). Walk straight ahead (S). Initially there is no path but, by a cairn on top of a rock, you can pick up a path – if you can't find this do not worry, just keep heading S. ▶

If you are lucky you might find some Edelweiss on the plateau.

When the path fades again, keep heading S towards the highest point in front of you. As you come up over a rise, you will see a cross straight ahead. This is the **Croix de la Salcette** (2331m, 2hr 50mins).

The **views from the cross** are immense: so are the sheer drops over the cliffs, so watch your step!

167

The Mont Brison Massif and the Onde Valley viewed from Croix de la Salcette

From the cross follow a faint grassy path to the SW. After a few minutes a large cairn can be seen on top of a rock: aim for this. If visibility is low, take great care as it would be easy to lose your way on the plateau and the cliffs are sheer. The path continues to the right of the cairn and bears round to the S. The path now begins its descent in earnest: it is extremely steep in places and a couple of sections require a little bit of light scrambling.

At a signpost (2063m), turn left and head downhill to the SE towards Bouchier. Eventually, the path becomes a track. Follow this track to a cairn on the right and a red and green arrow on a tree. Here leave the track onto a path. After another 10–15min arrive at a junction and turn left towards Bouchier.

After 5–10min arrive at a vehicle track. Turn left and arrive at **Bouchier** (3hr 45min). Walk between the old stone buildings until you emerge at the track you arrived on.

WALK 28
Cime de la Condamine

Start/finish	Small car park above the hamlet of les Combes (1870m, UTM 32T 308180 4973889)
Distance	14.5km
Ascent/descent	1150m
Grade	Very hard
Time	6hr 40min
Maximum altitude	2940m
Map	IGN 3536OT Briançon (1:25,000)
Refreshments	None
Access	From the bottom of Briançon take the D36 to Puy St André. Turn right at a cross and keep climbing. After a few minutes, at another junction, turn left, signposted to 'les Combes'. Pass through Puy Chalvin, where the tarred road gives way to gravel. After 10min drive through les Combes (1853m). A few hundred metres after the hamlet, reach a small parking area. Be careful not to miss this parking area: a deep gully in the road soon afterwards would not be passable by many cars.

This difficult route navigates two major cols, the Col de la Trancoulette and the Col de Vallouise, and climbs the magnificent Cime de la Condamine, the sentinel that dominates the Vallouise Valley. The broad summit is just a shade under 3000m and offers a spectacular 360° panorama. A tough descent through stunning scenery brings you to a pretty alpine lake surrounded by wild flowers. This is a fantastic route for those wanting a challenge.

It is a high-altitude walk, so save it for a fine day. The ascent to Cime de la Condamine is very steep and involves some light scrambling in places. The descent from the summit is also very steep, and large sections of the descent are without paths or waymarks. Accordingly, those who are not comfortable with navigation and map reading should perhaps avoid this walk. Those that do undertake it should not be disappointed.

From the parking area, head NW on the road. After 5–10min go through a barrier to reach a map on a board. Follow the track to the left of the board, heading uphill initially to the SW. The track quickly veers around to the NW and continues upwards. Soon the path begins to climb more steeply and shortly afterwards you arrive at a fork: take the left branch in the direction of 'Col de la Trancoulette'.

At another fork again turn left in the direction of 'Col de la Trancoulette'. The path bends to the left and starts to climb steeply up the face of the hillside through the trees. At a clearing, follow a grassy track towards the SW and then the S. Keep heading upwards along the path. Eventually, the path emerges from a group of trees into a

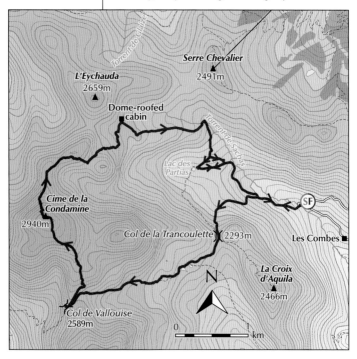

Mont Pelvoux and the Écrins National Park from the Col de Vallouise

gully. Turn right (S) to head up the gully – this is the steep final approach to **Col de la Trancoulette** (2293m, 1hr). ▶

From the col take the path to the right (SW), signposted 'Col de Vallouise'. The path contours around the hillside: directly ahead are the Tête des Lauzières and the mighty Mont Brison. After 10min the path passes to the N of a **pair of little lakes** (which are unnamed on the IGN map).

At the second lake, continue on the path as it contours around the hill to arrive at a little saddle to the SW. From the saddle, continue on the path as it heads W up into the valley. The path becomes faint in places as it crosses grassy areas. About 5–10min after the second lake, leave this path in favour of a faint path which heads up to the right. This often rocky path skirts the hillside well above the valley floor and continues generally W almost all the way to the Col de Vallouise. However, it would be easy to miss this junction. If you do, then it is relatively straightforward to proceed W up the valley floor instead, but here the path is at times non-existent or hard to discern: as long as you head generally W then you should stay on track.

The views from the col are beautiful but as you continue they will get even better.

Eventually the path arrives at **Col de Vallouise** (2589m, 2hr 10min), with spectacular views directly into the Écrins National Park.

From Col de Vallouise, retrace your steps for a few metres until the path splits at a cairn – take the left fork (NE). Keep on this path, following the cairns, pretty much all the way to the summit. Some 5–10min after Col de Vallouise, the path bears around to the N and climbs steeply across rocks.

Snow can remain here until early July and sometimes conceals the path.

At approximately 2700m arrive at a small plateau. ◄ Head N across the plateau (again there are cairns). Soon the path begins to climb steeply again as it heads up into a rocky outcrop. Where the path disappears, scramble up the last few metres over the outcrop. At the top of the outcrop, pick up the path again, now leading along the crest of a ridge towards the summit.

On a clear day, you will be rewarded with amazing 360° views which remain for the first part of the descent.

On the crest, where the path peters out again at a cairn, scramble up the slope to the NW to pick up the path again at the top. Follow the path and cairns to arrive at the broad summit of **Cime de la Condamine** (2940m, 3hr 35min). ◄

Cime de la Condamine in early summer as seen from near Lac des Partias

From the summit, head N in the direction of a cairn a few metres away, where you will pick up a stony path descending to the N. The path is very steep and covered with shale (so watch your footing).

The path descends Crête de Coste Groselière, heading N, and eventually passes down the right (E) flank of the ridge. Again, watch your footing as the path is steep and unstable in places. At a small saddle the path bears around to the NE, still on the right flank of the ridge.

When the path disappears at a small col, head NE (still along the right flank of the ridge). You may pick up the path again for a short distance but it is very faint. Soon the rocky terrain gives way to a predominantly grassy slope: head E down this, away from the ridge. As you descend, head straight towards a dome-shaped mountain: there is no path here and the grassy slope is steep in places.

Arriving at a small saddle below the dome-shaped mountain, turn left (NE) and descend down a gully through the rocks. ▸ The majority of the descent is without a path and is hard going in places (from time to time you may have to scramble downwards), but the views remain sublime throughout and you are unlikely to encounter anyone else.

Fabulous view from the summit of Cime de la Condamine

Take note here of a dome-roofed cabin ahead on the other side of the valley as you will use this for navigation later on.

When you see the **dome-roofed cabin** again, make for it (N or NE, depending upon exactly how far you have descended). Make sure you do not go too far down towards the NE because if you descend into the bottom of the valley further than required then you will have further to climb back up the other side towards the cabin.

Climb over a small rise and descend briefly into the valley to the N, still in the direction of the cabin. At the top of the rise, a second cabin with a pitched roof will also come into view. At the bottom of the valley, cross a stream and climb the other side to arrive at the dome-roofed cabin (5hr 10min).

From the cabin, head SE along a broad grassy whale back ridge (on which the dome shaped cabin sits) – do not take the path that crosses over the ridge and descends its N side. As the ridge approaches some unusually shaped rocky cliffs it descends to a small saddle. Turn left here and pick up a faint path descending NE. Keep just to the N of the cliffs and soon the path bears round to the E. When the path disappears, remain just to the N of the jagged cliffs.

When the cliffs end, descend E to a small lake (5hr 35min). Here bear left, heading NE, and descend to the left of a rocky outcrop into Ravin Mélivrin. At the bottom of the ravine, cross a stream and pick up a small path on the other side. Soon the path crosses back to the S side of the ravine.

Now straight ahead you should see Col de Trancoulette again. After a few minutes, when the path forks, take the right fork to **Lac des Partias** (2104m, 6hr).

Be aware that this junction is easy to miss – if you do miss it, then follow the main path until it descends to a signpost. Turn right here (signposted 'Lac des Partias'). After a few metres, ignore a track heading off on the left and keep straight ahead to arrive at the lake.

From the lake, head E on a track past some wooden buildings. At a signpost, keep straight ahead and follow the path all the way back to the car park (6hr 40min).

WALK 29

La Croix d'Aquila

Start/finish	Small car park above the hamlet of les Combes (1870m, UTM 32T 308180 4973889)
Distance	12km
Ascent/descent	720m
Grade	Medium
Time	4hr 10min
Maximum altitude	2466m
Map	IGN 3536OT Briançon (1:25,000)
Refreshments	None
Access	From the bottom of Briançon take the D36 to Puy St André. Turn right at a cross and keep climbing. After a few minutes, at another junction, turn left (signposted 'les Combes'). Soon afterwards, pass through the village of Puy Chalvin and then the tarred road ends and you continue on a gravel road. After 10min pass through the hamlet of les Combes (1853m). A few hundred metres after the hamlet, reach a small parking area. Be careful not to go past this parking area as there is a deep gully in the road soon afterwards which would not be passable by many cars.

This walk offers a day of easily accessible alpine scenery – a beautiful col, a precipitous peak, green pastures (with the requisite cows and bells) and scented larch forests. As the crow flies you are close to Briançon, however, it feels like you are in the middle of nowhere. It is one of the author's favourites and, if you have a head for heights, the exposure at the Croix d'Aquila is to be savoured.

The walk is on clear paths except for the descent from the Col de la Trancoulette, which is across grassy slopes.

From the parking area, head NW on the road. After 5–10min go through a barrier and arrive at a map on

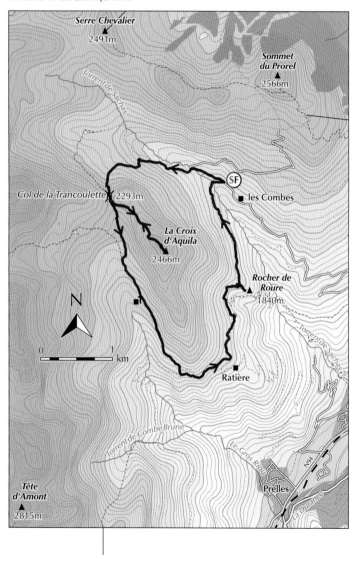

board. Follow the track to the left of the board, heading uphill initially to the SW. The track quickly veers around to the NW and continues upwards. Soon the path begins to climb more steeply and shortly afterwards you arrive at a fork – take the left branch in the direction of 'Col de la Trancoulette'.

At another fork, again turn left in the direction of 'Col de la Trancoulette'. The path bends to the left and starts to climb steeply up the face of the hillside through the trees. Arrive in a clearing and then follow a grassy track towards the SW and then the S. Keep heading upwards along the path. Eventually, the path emerges from a group of trees into a gully. Turn right (S) to head up the gully – this is the steep final approach to **Col de la Trancoulette** (2293m, 1hr). ▸

There are fine views from here but the best is yet to come.

From the col take the path to the left (SE) to climb up the Crête du Dos d'Ane de Passage towards the Croix d'Aquila. As you climb, you will see, over the other side of the valley to your right, Mont Brison and the Col de Vallouise.

As you arrive on top of the ridge, new views to the E present themselves. Soon the path slips left off to the E side of the ridge and continues climbing. About 1hr 35min from the start arrive at the **Croix d'Aquila** (2466m).

The Croix d'Aquila with Briançon in the background

Viewpoint on top of Rocher de Roure (1840m)

The **360° views** are astounding. This is the high point of the walk and on a fine day it is a fantastic place to pause for a picnic: but the drops are sheer so take care while you are taking photos.

To descend, retrace your steps back down the ridge towards Col de la Trancoulette. You should arrive back at the col 25min after leaving the cross.

For the next part of the walk it is time for some minor 'bushwhacking' because, although a path is indicated on the IGN map, it is difficult to discern on the ground. Consequently, it is easier to just walk over the grass rather than spend too much time searching for faint paths. The grassy terrain is steep in places but otherwise not too challenging.

From the col initially head SSE down across the grassy slope. To assist with navigation, you should aim for two very large boulders which you will see directly ahead of you, downhill. Use the contours of the terrain to work your way down to these boulders. At times you may be able to pick up a faint path, but don't worry if you cannot: as long as you keep heading towards the two boulders you will not go far wrong.

Pass to the right of the two boulders and keep ahead to the SE towards another big boulder on a small grassy hill with a path running to the right of it. Keep close to the shale slopes on your left. Pick up the path, pass the boulder and continue SE. When the path disappears, keep heading SE still staying close to the mountains to your left – do not descend into the valley on your right. Eventually, you will see an old farm building with a cross behind it. Make for this (SSE). Arrive at the building and the cross 25min from the Col de la Trancoulette.

Pass to the left of the cross and keep ahead on a track descending roughly S. After about 15min on this track, reach a junction and keep right. At the next junction (at another cross), turn left onto another track. Almost immediately after the cross, ignore a rough track heading downhill on the right.

After about 5min, at a signpost where the track loops around to the right, leave the main track and follow a forest track on the left in the direction of 'Rocher de Roure'. Shortly afterwards, leave the forest track in favour of a path heading down the hill to the right (signposted 'Rocher de Roure'). Head through larch forest and at another junction keep straight ahead, again towards 'Rocher de Roure'. Finally, the path climbs for 5min to arrive at a signpost on top of **Rocher de Roure** (1840m, 3hr 25min). Turn right and walk along the top of the ridge for a few minutes to reach a **very fine viewpoint** on the precipitous edge of a very high cliff.

To continue the walk, retrace your steps from the viewpoint and return to the signpost. Keep straight ahead (signposted 'les Combes'). Almost immediately the path splits – take the right fork to follow a path which undulates across the face of the slope (neither gaining nor losing much height). On the right you will see **les Combes**.

At a junction keep left and climb briefly – do not take the path on the right, which descends into the valley. The path eventually arrives onto a grassy track – turn right. Shortly afterwards, the track crosses a small river, bends to the right and climbs, and a few minutes later meets the gravel road you arrived on. Turn left to reach the parking area (4hr 10min).

GUISANE VALLEY

The area around l'Aiguillette du Lauzet is a
highlight of the region (Walks 37 and 38)

WALK 30

Briançon and Fort des Salettes

Start/finish	Briançon (1332m, UTM 32T 314015 4974701)
Distance	7km
Ascent/descent	350m
Grade	Easy
Time	2hr 10min
Maximum altitude	1533m
Map	IGN 3536OT Briançon (1:25,000)
Refreshments	Briançon
Access	Start from the car park on the N94 at the northern edge of Briançon's old town

The old city of Briançon has many interesting sights and this easy walk provides the perfect introduction. The route takes you past many of Vauban's military buildings, including the well preserved Fort des Salettes. It also directs you through the heart of the old town, from where you could visit many other historic fortifications or take a stroll around the amazing city walls. Finally, you could stop for a drink or a meal in one of Briançon's many cafés or restaurants or while away a few hours browsing in the interesting shops.

The well preserved walls of Briançon with Fort des Salettes in the background

From the car park head N and cross the main road. Opposite the car park is a little street (at a fountain) called Chemin des Salettes: head up this street to the NE. After a few minutes, at a junction of tracks, turn right. Keep on this path to **Fort des Salettes** (1450m, 20min).

To the W of the fort, take a path which heads uphill to the N. After a few minutes, at a junction, keep right towards 'Rocher de l'Ombre'. At the next fork keep

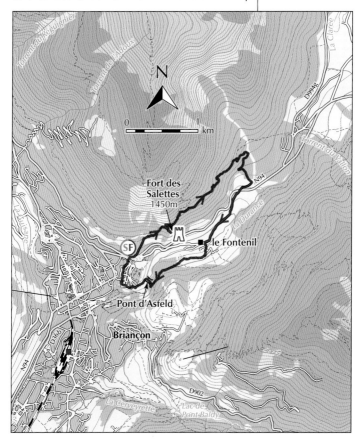

FORT DES SALETTES

Designed by Vauban but built after his death between 1709 and 1712, Fort des Salettes is situated on a convenient plateau overlooking the N side of the old town of Briançon. The fort consists of a robust keep, or redoute, surrounded by a moat. The drawbridge over the moat can still be seen today. It was modified between 1835 and 1855, when new stronger walls around the original keep were added.

The fort is generally closed to the public but visits can be organised by contacting the Service Patrimoine of Briançon on tel +33(0)4 92 20 29 49 or patrimoine@mairie-briancon.fr.

right. Follow the path until it arrives at another junction of tracks: turn right again, in the direction of a sign to 'Briançon par le Fontenil', and descend on this track all the way to the main road (**N94**) (1hr 10min).

Cross over the N94 in the direction of a sign to 'Briançon par le Fontenil' and follow a small road SW down to the village of **le Fontenil**. In the village turn left to cross a road bridge across the River Durance. Then keep straight ahead up the road (initially S). Where the road bears round to the left at a hairpin bend, take a little path off to the right in the apex of the hairpin. Shortly afterwards, this path joins a track: turn right along the track.

At a fork keep left. Soon after this, leave the track in favour of a path to the right (at a signpost towards 'Briançon par Pont d'Asfeld'). There are a number of interlinking paths here – to avoid confusion, from the signpost head across a little field and follow a path SW into the trees. There are red and white waymarks from time to time to mark the correct route – keep following these but remember that, as always, a red and white 'X' indicates the wrong route.

Pont d'Asfeld was completed in 1734 and is 60m above the River Durance.

When you arrive at a junction of wide tracks, keep right downhill, following a sign towards 'Pont d'Asfeld'. Soon after this, arrive at **Pont d'Asfeld** (1290m, 1hr 40min). ◀

Cross over the bridge and turn left up a track. Soon afterwards, enter the gates of **Briançon** (Porte de la

Durance) and turn left along Rue Aspirant Jan to walk around the city walls. After 5min, at Place Médecin Générale Blanchard, find Grande Rue on the right – this is Briançon's main street. Head up this street, where there are plenty of restaurants and interesting shops. At the top of the street, head through some arches in a building to arrive at another set of city gates (Porte de Pignerol). Head through the gates and turn right to arrive back at the car park (2hr 10min).

Pont d'Asfeld with Fort des Salettes in the background

WALK 31
La Croix de Toulouse

Start/finish	Briançon (1332m, UTM 32T 314015 4974701)
Distance	9.5km
Ascent/descent	650m
Grade	Medium
Time	3hr 10min
Maximum altitude	1973m
Map	IGN 3536OT Briançon (1:25,000)
Refreshments	Briançon
Access	Start from the car park on the N94 at the northern edge of Briançon's old town

This super little walk involves a straightforward climb to an amazing viewpoint, giving a bird's eye of Briançon and its surrounds. Clearly visible are each of the five valleys which form the spokes of the cartwheel which has Briançon as its hub. And since many of Briançon's forts can be spotted, it is also one of the best viewpoints from which to gain an appreciation of Briançon's defences and military past.

The route starts from Briançon's old town, so it can be easily combined with a window shopping session, a meal or simply a stroll through the atmospheric streets and alleys.

From the car park head N and cross the main road. Opposite the car park there is a little street (at a fountain) called Chemin des Salettes: head up this street to the NE. After a few minutes, at a junction of tracks, turn right. Keep on this path until you arrive at **Fort des Salettes** (1450m, 20min). For further information on Fort des Salettes see Walk 30.

To the W of the Fort, take a path which heads uphill to the N (signposted 'Croix de Toulouse'). After a few minutes, at a junction, turn left (again signposted to 'Croix de Toulouse'). ◄ Here and there you should spot red and white waymarks on the trees to guide you.

As you climb, the views into the Durance Valley get better and better: many forts are visible, as is the Pont d'Asfeld spanning the gorge below Briançon's old town.

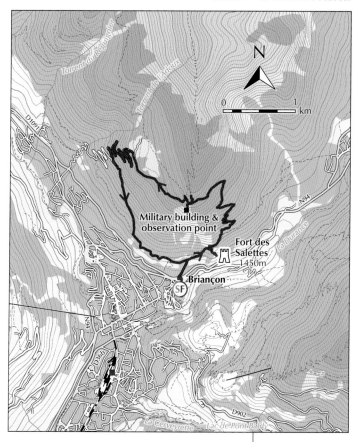

After 5min turn left uphill at another junction (signposted 'Croix de Toulouse'). The path now climbs in earnest and skirts around the E side of the slope. At the next junction, turn left (signposted 'Croix de Toulouse') and continue uphill.

Eventually, reach an **old military building and observation point** (1hr 25min, 1973m).

From the observation point, each of **Briançon's five valleys** can be clearly seen as can an impressive number of the city's major forts, including Fort de Salettes, Fort du Château, Fort Dauphin, Fort des Trois Têtes, Fort du Randouillet, Fort d'Anjou, Fort de l'Infernet, Fort de la Croix de Bretagne and la Grande Maye (see Walk 18).

Take the path heading N on the W side of the military building. Almost immediately, at a fork, keep left to descend on a small road (D232T). Shortly afterwards, at a signpost, leave the road in favour of a little path on the left heading downhill initially to the S. ◄

Take care as it would be easy to miss this signpost.

After about 10min from the signpost is another sign (1850m): keep straight ahead (signposted to 'Briançon par le chemin de la Racine').

Reaching the D232T again, 2hr 5min from the start, turn left and descend on the road which snakes downwards by way of a number of hairpins.

Briançon and the Fort de Château as viewed on the descent from la Croix de Toulouse

Just up on the left there is a large grassy plateau which would make a super **viewpoint for a picnic**. As you descend, the views into the Guisane Valley are magnificent.

A view of the Guisane Valley from nearby la Croix de Toulouse

In the apex of the eighth hairpin, 2hr 30min from the start, leave the road in favour of a little path on the left. Take care on this path as it is slightly eroded in places. At a fork, turn right (signposted 'Briançon'). Shortly afterwards the path joins a track: turn left, still signposted 'Briançon'.

After 3hr arrive back at the junction you passed earlier (before Fort des Salettes) – turn right and descend to arrive back at the car park (3hr 10min).

WALK 32
Circuit of le Grand Area

Start/finish	Bergerie Saint Joseph near Col de Granon (2171m, UTM 32T 309495 4982277)
Distance	15.75km
Ascent/descent	800m
Grade	Hard
Time	6hr
Maximum altitude	2483m
Map	IGN 3536OT Briançon (1:25,000) and IGN 3535OT Névache (1:25,000)
Refreshments	Refuge de Buffère
Access	From Briançon travel NW along the D1091 to the W side of St Chaffrey. At a roundabout with an old cable car in the middle of it, turn right (signposted 'St Chaffrey'). Pass through St Chaffrey, and after a few minutes turn right onto 'Route du Granon' (signposted 'Col de Granon' and 'Villard-Laté'). Pass through 'Villard-Laté' on the D234T. 8km from Villard-Laté, at a right-hand hairpin, take a track on the left to Bergerie Saint Joseph. There is plenty of parking here.

This circuit of one of the Guisane's most recognisable peaks explores both sides of the ridge dividing the Guisane and Clarée Valleys. The scenery is out of this world. The route crosses two beautiful and very different cols and passes two exquisite Alpine lakes. There are also pretty pastures, rivers and wild flowers throughout. Half of the walk is on the Guisane side of the ridge, with spectacular views S into the Écrins National Park. The other half is on the Clarée Valley side with its different, but equally wonderful, views to the N.

Despite the long length of the walk it is not too difficult, largely because the altitude gain is staggered. A gentle climb at the start as you ascend Col de Buffère is followed, some hours later, by a second, slightly longer and steeper climb up to Porte de Cristol. The walk is mostly on clear paths and tracks, except on the Côte Rouge, which is rocky in places. Navigation is largely straightforward: however, on the Côte Rouge there are a few places where the path is hard to follow – fortunately, there are pink waymarks to assist.

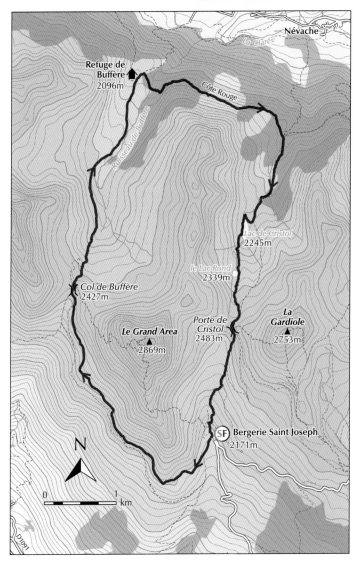

From the Bergerie Saint Joseph, take the track heading SW (signposted 'Col de Buffère'). The first few km are on a balcony which climbs gently and overlooks the Guisane Valley as it winds its way around the S face of le Grand Area.

After 30min, arrive at a fork – keep right (signposted 'Col de Buffère') onto a track which is followed all the way to the Col de Buffère. Just below the col, at a junction of tracks by some old ruins, keep right to arrive at the broad **Col de Buffère** (2427m, 1hr 20min).

From the col, follow a path to the N towards a post with a red and white waymark on it. Soon the path makes its way NE as it descends through a green valley which is filled with the vibrant pink Alpenrose in July. The path continues broadly N to arrive at **Refuge de Buffère** (2096m, 2hr 25min).

> **Refuge de Buffère** is a fine place for lunch or to stay the night. It is staffed from mid-June until mid-September and has 30 dormitory places. Tel +33 (0)4 92 21 34 03, www.refugebuffere.com.

Keep heading NE past the refuge and after a few minutes, at a signpost, turn right onto a grassy path (signposted 'Névache–Côte Rouge'). After 5min, where the path forks, go left to cross a wooden footbridge. This is the start of the **Côte Rouge**, so-called because in the autumn the hillside is a vibrant red colour. There are some pink spots on the rocks to guide you along this undulating path which is rocky in places and slightly tricky underfoot. Soon you will see the town of Névache below.

Eventually, the path climbs a small hill, descends the other side and arrives at a signpost (3hr 40min) – keep straight ahead. Shortly afterwards, cross a river on a footbridge and then turn right and head uphill (SW) on a path (signposted 'Porte de Cristol').

Stay on this path (broadly SW) all the way to Lac de Cristol. Just before the lake, there is a junction – keep right to arrive at the gorgeous **Lac de Cristol** (2245m, 4hr 15min). From here, follow a path around to the W side of the lake and then keep on it to the S.

At the SW tip of the lake, pick up a path heading upwards to the SW – ignore any offshoots from the main path as these are dead ends. The path climbs to **Lac Rond** (2339m, 4hr 50min). Pass to the left (E) of the lake and keep climbing to the S.

Not far from the top of the ridge to the S, arrive at a junction of paths with a signpost – turn right and make the final ascent up to **Porte de Cristol** (2483m, 5hr 20min). Cross over the col and descend on a path to the S.

After a few minutes, arrive at a junction of paths with a signpost – turn right and descend steeply at first. After a few more minutes, the path levels off slightly and descends gently to the S. At a junction of paths and tracks, head straight across the junction and descend on a path to the SW. Shortly afterwards, the path meets a track – turn left. After a few metres, cross a small ravine and, immediately afterwards, leave the track for a path on the right. The path winds its way down through the grassy valley.

Eventually, when the path descends to a track, just above **Bergerie Saint Joseph**, turn right. Shortly afterwards, take a path on the left to descend to the start (6hr).

Vibrant pink Alpenrose fills the slopes in July

WALK 33

La Grande Peyrolle by the Crête de Peyrolle

Start/finish	Col de Granon (2404m, UTM 32T 311607 4981605)
Distance	10.25km
Ascent/descent	570m
Grade	Medium
Time	3hr 40min
Maximum altitude	2645m
Map	IGN 3536OT Briançon (1:25,000)
Refreshments	The buvette at the Col de Granon should be open during July and August
Access	From Briançon travel NW along the D1091 to the W side of St Chaffrey. At a roundabout with an old cable car in the middle of it, turn right (signposted 'St Chaffrey') and pass through St Chaffrey. After a few minutes, turn right onto 'Route du Granon' (signposted 'Col de Granon' and 'Villard-Laté'). Pass through 'Villard-Laté' on the D234T. Keep on up the D234T all the way to the large parking area at the top of the col, passing some old military barracks on the way.

This unforgettable ridge walk has non-stop views. The ridge is narrow and exposed on both sides: you'll need a head for heights and it's best avoided on very windy days. The route is undulating so the height gain and loss are greater than they might appear from a map. Do not let this put you off as this walk is one of the finest.

From the car park at the col, initially head S, following the sign for the 'Crête de Peyrolle par Croix de la Cime'. Shortly afterwards, arrive at an observation post which gives the names of the many visible peaks.

> The **peaks** you can see from here include the famous la Meije, Barre des Écrins and Mont Pelvoux, all of which are in the Écrins National Park.

From the observation post, head along the path (initially to the SE). Just over 10min from the start, arrive a fork: you can take either the left or the right fork. ▶ Descend briefly and, before a pair of buildings, the path forks. Take the left fork to climb up the side of the hill to your left.

About 30min from the start, arrive at **Col de Barteaux** (2380m). Follow the sign for 'la Grande Peyrolle' and climb the clear path up onto the ridge. As you climb, the views open up on both sides. From the ridge you will see the Clarée Valley to the E. The path snakes its way along the crest of the ridge. There are steep drops on either side of the ridge and the exposure is thrilling.

About 35min from the col, arrive at the **Croix de la Cime** (2603m). You will see your path snaking upwards ahead of you. The descent from the cross is steep, with plenty of loose rock, so watch your step. The path ahead up along the ridge is faint in places but there are pink markers on the rocks to guide you.

At the top of the next rise you will see la Grande Peyrolle ahead of you and the Crête de la Charmette extending down to the N. Descend again briefly and

Straight ahead the Crête de Peyrolle stands proud. To the right you will see Briançon and beyond.

The Croix de la Cime (2603m) towers above the Clarée Valley

To the S you can see la Petite Peyrolle, the Serre des Aigles and the path for the descent, zigzagging below.

keep following the path ahead along the side of the mountain. You then descend down onto a small saddle at which there is a fork. Take the left fork up face of la Grande Peyrolle (or the right fork instead if you wish to avoid the peak). Climb until you reach a cairn, indicating that you have reached the top of **la Grande Peyrolle** (2645m), around 35min from the Croix de la Cime. ◄

Retrace your steps back down from the peak until you come to the point where the path loops round to the right (W). Instead of following the path, leave it here and head straight down the mountain to the S. Descend directly onto the path below you and turn left to follow the path across the face of the mountain and then down to a saddle.

Shortly after the saddle, arrive at a fork and take the right branch (indicated by a pink arrow) to descend. About 10min after the fork, the path comes to a small stream (which may be dry). Do not cross the stream but instead follow the path round to the right. Shortly afterwards, the path crosses a gully and then heads W across the S face of the **Crête de Peyrolle**. The path crosses shale in places so watch your footing. ◄

There are fabulous views to the left into the Écrins National Park.

About 30min after the gully, reach a couple of forks. Ignore the paths heading downhill to the left and keep

The Crête de Peyrolle seen from near Col de Barteaux

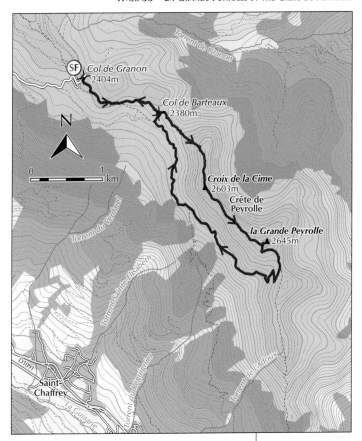

right. After another 10min, arrive at a signpost labelled 'les Sagnes'. Keep on the path straight ahead in the direction of 'Col de Granon'.

At another sign labelled 'Côte de la Fleur (2370m)', turn right in the direction of the 'Col de Barteaux'. At the col turn left along the path (which is the same one you travelled on earlier), and follow it all the way back to **Col de Granon**.

WALK 34
Grand Lac de l'Oule

Start/finish	Col de Granon (2404m, UTM 32T 311607 4981605)
Distance	6.5km
Ascent/descent	290m
Grade	Easy
Time	2hr 20min
Maximum altitude	2564m
Map	IGN 3536OT Briançon (1:25,000)
Refreshments	The buvette at the Col de Granon should be open during July and August
Access	From Briançon travel NW along the D1091 to the W side of St Chaffrey. At a roundabout with an old cable car in the middle of it, turn right (signposted 'St Chaffrey') through St Chaffrey. A few minutes afterwards, turn right onto 'Route du Granon' (signposted 'Col de Granon' and 'Villard-Laté'). Pass through 'Villard-Laté' on the D234T. Keep on up the D234T all the way to the large parking area at the top of the col, passing some old military barracks on the way.

This very beautiful route is entirely above the tree line and allows you to enjoy high alpine scenery with only a modicum of effort. Although the walk is short there is plenty to see, passing two cols and a magnificent lake. If you only have a half day then this makes for a superb outing at high altitude.

The walk is entirely on clear paths and neither navigation nor terrain should pose any difficulties. The small altitude gain/loss makes this a fantastic walk for families.

From the car park, walk a short distance back down the road and take a track on the right heading NW (signposted 'Col des Cibières'). The path passes some old military barracks. After a few minutes, leave the track in favour of a path on the right (signposted 'Lac de l'Oule') which climbs gently to the NW. ◄

The views of the Écrins National Park are magnificent.

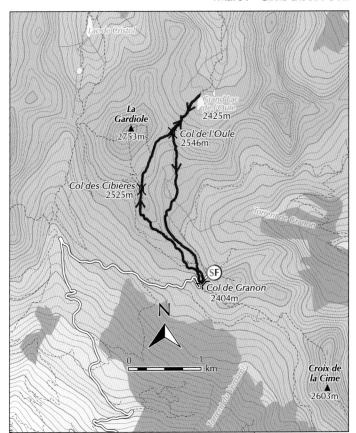

When the path bears around to the N, you will see the peak of le Grand Area to the W. Eventually, arrive at **Col des Cibières** (2525m, 35min) where there is a junction of paths: take the right fork (N) (signposted 'Col de l'Oule').

After another 15min, at a junction of paths with some cairns, keep right and descend briefly to the NE. The path then climbs gently for a few minutes to arrive at

199

The lovely Grand Lac d'Oule is a fantastic spot for a picnic

Col de l'Oule (2546m, 1hr), which has some very beautiful views. Cross over the col and descend to the NE on a path towards the lake, which you will now see below you.

Arrive at **Grand Lac de l'Oule** (2425m, 1hr 20min).

You will not want to rush away from **Grand Lac de l'Oule**, and it is very tempting to dip your feet in the emerald green water while admiring your surroundings.

From the lake, retrace your steps to climb back up to the **Col de l'Oule** (1hr 40min). At the signpost on the col, bear left (S) to head back towards the Col de Granon (which you can see ahead) on a path down through a grassy valley. As you descend, views down into the Clarée Valley open up.

At a fork in the track, near the ridge on the right, keep right, follow the path heading along the flank of the ridge to arrive back at the **Col de Granon** (2hr 20min).

WALK 35

La Cime des Conchiers

Start/finish	Le Monêtier-les-Bains (1495m, UTM 32T 303259 4983504)
Distance	7.75km
Ascent/descent	485m
Grade	Medium
Time	3hr
Maximum altitude	1935m
Map	IGN 3536OT Briançon (1:25,000)
Refreshments	Le Monêtier-les-Bains
Access	From Briançon head NW on the D1091. Pass through le Monêtier-les-Bains: as you leave the town there is a car park on the right named 'P8 Pommier'.

If you want to get into the high mountains with relatively little effort then this walk is for you. It starts at the lovely thermal spa town of le Monêtier-les-Bains, climbs through pristine aromatic forest, makes a high altitude traverse across a mountain plateau and visits two deserted alpine hamlets. There are stunning views into the Guisane Valley throughout.

Navigation poses little difficulty provided you follow the pink waymarks.

Walk up the road at the N side of the car park and, almost immediately, meet another road (Rue St-Joseph). Turn right (E) towards the town. On the right you will see an unusual building with 13 sides called la Rotonde.

THE THERMAL BATHS OF LE MONÊTIER-LES-BAINS

La Rotonde was a 'pavillon des buveurs' (literally 'drinkers' lodge') dating from the early part of the 18th century. It is one of two sources of hot spring water used in the thermal baths after which le Monêtier-les-Bains is named. The water is thought to originate from a geological fault and, by the time it bubbles up from the ground, it has a temperature of around 39°C.

The water is said to have numerous health benefits and the ability to cure a variety of complaints, including rheumatism and skin conditions. The positive effects of the thermal springs have been known since Roman times but it was not until 1715 that spa baths were officially established. La Rotonde was built around this time, and throughout the 18th century the baths were used by wealthy travellers, wounded soldiers and locals alike. Around the middle of the 19th century the baths, which had fallen into disrepair, were redeveloped and a number of hotels were built nearby. The town was originally known as 'Monêtier de Briançon': it changed its name in 1893.

These days the baths are housed in a modern complex to the S of the town. The views from the glamorous building are stunning and can be enjoyed while soaking, indoors or outdoors, in a selection of pools, jacuzzis and saunas. www.lesgrandsbains.fr tel +33 (0)4 92 40 00 00.

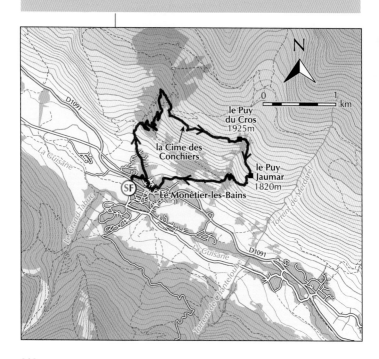

Statue of a Bouquetin in the centre of le Monêtier-les-Bains

After a few minutes, arrive at another car park (named 'P9 Conchiers'). Turn left here along 'Chemin du Puy Chevalier'. At another car park, keep ahead on the road which soon becomes a rocky track. ▸

About 20min from the start, arrive at a signpost at a fork (1610m). Turn right (signposted 'Col de Buffère') and keep climbing. After a few minutes, arrive at another sign for 'la Cime des Conchiers'. Keep climbing along the path following the pink waymarks on the rocks.

Shortly afterwards, turn right at another fork by a signpost ('Forêt Domaniale de la Guisane'). Again, if in doubt, follow the pink waymarks. After a few more minutes, at another signpost (1660m), turn left towards 'Col de Buffère', still following the pink waymarks. The path climbs steadily as it zigzags through the forest.

There is a path to the right of the track which may be more comfortable to walk on.

203

Arrive at a junction (approximately 1835m) 1hr from the start, and turn right (pink waymarks). Shortly afterwards, ignore a small path to the left and keep to the right (pink waymarks).

Eventually, at a cabin, turn right (signposted 'Puy du Cros'). Shortly afterwards the path exits the trees, giving expansive views into the Guisane Valley. This is the start of the traverse across **la Cime des Conchiers**.

Follow the signposts to 'Puy du Cros' to arrive at the deserted hamlet of **le Puy du Cros** (1925m, 1hr 40min), with its little chapel. From here, follow a sign for 'Monêtier par le Puy Jaumar' and pass to the left of the chapel.

Arrive at **le Puy Jaumar** (1820m, 1hr 55min), another deserted hamlet. Here, at a signpost, follow the path around to the right passing to the left of the little chapel and to the right of a cross. Once again, pink waymarks will guide you.

Arriving at a fork (1630m, 2hr 30min), turn left and keep descending towards le Monêtier-les-Bains.

An icy winter landscape seen from Cime de Conchiers

After 10min arrive at another junction (1504m) and turn right. When the path arrives at a road, turn right and, shortly afterwards, keep straight ahead on a path. Where the path meets a track, turn left to descend into **le Monêtier-les-Bains**.

> From here, you can pick your own route to wander through **le Monêtier-les-Bains** if you prefer. There are plenty of restaurants and cafes at which you can rest weary legs.
>
> If, however, you simply wish to return to the start, then the description below takes you there on a pleasant route which passes through the church square and some of the town's ancient back alleys.

When the path arrives at a small street, turn right. Shortly afterwards, turn left along 'Rue Saint-Alexis'. At the end of this street, turn right to arrive in the church square. Keep straight ahead with the church on your left. Before the end of the square, turn right onto 'Rue de la Fontaine'. Shortly afterwards, turn left just before a fountain (there is a signpost behind a wall for 'Au fil de l'eau') to take a path between buildings and a wall. The path twists and turns back to the car park ('P9 Conchiers') which you passed earlier. Turn left and shortly afterwards arrive back at the start (3hr).

WALK 36

Lac de Combeynot

Start/finish	Car park at les Boussardes (near le Lauzet) (1626m, UTM 32T 300293 4987302)
Distance	8.25km
Ascent/descent	930m
Grade	Hard
Time	3hr 50min
Maximum altitude	2555m
Map	IGN 3436ET Meije Pelvoux (1:25,000)
Refreshments	Le Lauzet has a restaurant
Access	From Briançon head NW on the D1091. About 5km after le Monêtier-les-Bains, take a small road on the left (not signposted) and descend towards les Boussardes. At the river, turn left across a small bridge then immediately right into a small parking area. The road off the D1091 is easy to miss so if you cannot find it then the head into the village of le Lauzet. At the bottom of the village by the river, turn left and work your way SE until you come to the bridge at les Boussardes.

This walk climbs through a shady, fragrant forest and emerges into the rugged and beautiful Vallon de Fontenil. It then ascends to a remote mountain lake in the Écrins National Park. The route is straightforward except for a tricky rocky section close to the lake.

From the car park, walk back towards the bridge and then up the road a short distance towards les Boussardes. Almost immediately, take the small track to the right of some information boards on the right and start your climb. After 10min there is a sign marking the entrance to the Écrins National Park.

Shortly afterwards, at a signpost, turn left in the direction of 'Lac de Combeynot'. After about 20min, the path enters some trees and works its way upwards on a rocky

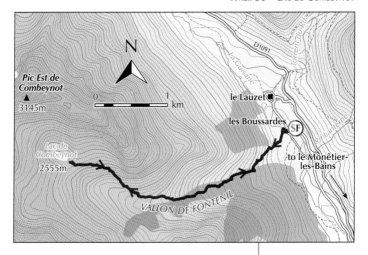

path which is faint in places. As you climb deeper into the Vallon du Fontenil, the trees start to thin. In autumn the myrtille bushes here turn red, and in the summer

Ascending through the Vallon du Fontenil towards Lac de Combeynot

there are plenty of myrtille berries which are related to the blueberry.

After 1hr 10min the path arrives alongside a huge field of boulders and skirts to the N of it. Soon there are some very steep sections as the path climbs up a series of rocky steps and then over rocks and shale. The path is hard to discern in places – if in doubt, keep heading uphill to the NW. You should also see a few blue waymarks on the rocks to guide you and, later on, some yellow arrows.

Eventually, the path levels out and heads W across the face of the slope. Finally, pass a couple of large cairns to reach **Lac de Combeynot** (2555m, 2hr 20min).

> **Lac de Combeynot** is situated in a rocky cirque, and if you arrive early you may see some Chamois or Bouquetin.
>
> If you wish to extend the walk, there is a path snaking upwards to the right of the lake which heads to Pic Est de Combeynot (3145m).

To descend, simply retrace your steps back down to the car park (3hr 50min). As you descend there are fantastic views into the Guisane Valley, with l'Aiguillette du Lauzet directly in front.

L'Aiguillette du Lauzet as viewed on the descent

WALK 37

Les Arêtes de la Bruyère

Start/finish	Le Pont de l'Alpe (1710m, UTM 32T 300338 4988118)
Distance	9.75km
Ascent/descent	734m
Grade	Hard
Time	4hr 25min
Maximum altitude	2440m
Map	IGN 3436ET Meije Pelvoux (1:25,000) or IGN 3535OT Névache (1:25,000)
Refreshments	None
Access	From Briançon head NW on the D1091. Shortly after the village of le Lauzet, arrive at le Pont de l'Alpe. There is little else here except for an auberge. Cross the bridge and immediately afterwards there is a parking area on the right.

If you have a head for heights then this walk should not be missed: it is not the longest, but certainly among the best of the area's routes. Indeed in good weather it could earn a place in many people's top ten walks anywhere, with a stunning alpine hamlet, striking jagged peaks and one of the finest lakes in the Alps. Added to that are the colours – in spring the blue and yellow carpet of flowers is very special and in autumn the yellows, golds and reds of the trees are unforgettable.

The route is mostly on good paths. However the climb up to le Grand Lac is very steep. The last section also involves a short scramble up a rocky face using fixed cables for assistance. There is no alternative route: for some this will be the highlight of the route but, for the more timid, it could prove something of an ordeal.

From the car park, walk back across the bridge in the direction of Briançon and immediately turn left up a track (signposted 'l'Alpe du Lauzet'). After a few minutes, at a junction, turn left (signposted 'Roche Robert').

Le Grand Lac with les Arêtes de la Bruyère

After another few minutes, at a hairpin bend, ignore a small path to the left and continue up the main path to the right.

Where the path meets a track, turn left and continue climbing to arrive at the beautifully situated hamlet of **l'Alpe du Lauzet** (1940m, 30min). A few minutes later, the track arrives at a footbridge – cross over the bridge and just afterwards, at a fork, take the right branch. The path heads around the W of **les Arêtes de la Bruyère**. ◀

As you continue to the NW, the large mountain up ahead is Roche Colombe.

The path arrives alongside a river and then ascends over rocks – this is a little tricky in places and the path is faint but just keep heading N and stay to the right of the stream. There is also a path on the left-hand side of the stream which you could take but the views are better to the right of the stream. As you descend off a grassy spur, the path begins to climb (N) up into a mountain cirque which is covered with wild flowers in spring.

On arrival at a rocky ravine, continue N up it on a rocky, but relatively well defined, path. The path zigzags up the face of the slopes and the further you climb the steeper it gets.

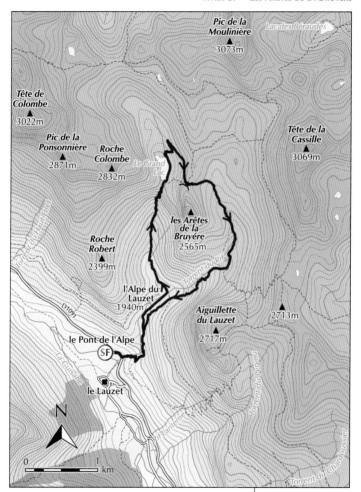

Eventually, the path ends at a rock face with steel cables bolted into it (1hr 30min). Put your walking poles away here because you will need both hands free to scramble up the rocks using the cables to assist you. Be careful as a fall here could have serious consequences.

After an exhilarating climb on the cables, reach a small col (1hr 40min) and take a moment here to savour the mountain landscape to the S. To the N another treat awaits you: **le Grand Lac** (2282m, 1hr 45min).

As you climb the views into the Écrins National Park are sublime. Les Arêtes de la Bruyère are close by to the S.

Head N towards the lake (which makes a super picnic spot) and then take the path which heads N around the E fringe of the lake. Towards the N side of the lake, the path starts to zigzag up the grassy slope to the NE (away from the lake). ◀

Eventually, near a cairn on top of a rock (2hr), the path arrives at another well defined path (the GR57). Turn right onto this path (SE). Keep climbing to arrive at a **col**, the high point of the day (2440m, 2hr 30min).

Making the exhilarating climb up the section of steel cables

From here, take a path which runs initially SE (signposted 'l'Alpe du Lauzet'). The path then descends E into a valley and eventually, bears around to the S. When the path drops down to a stream near a cairn (3hr), ford the stream and continue S on the path. The path is slightly faint in places.

The path passes close to les Arêtes de la Bruyère

When the path arrives at a signpost (3hr 15min), take the path headed down to the W (signposted 'l'Alpe du Lauzet'). Soon the path bears around to the S to arrive back at **l'Alpe du Lauzet** (3hr 45min). ▸

From here, keep heading downhill on a path that runs SW, to the left of the little church. Follow this path all the way down to the track you climbed on earlier. Head down the track and retrace your steps back to le Pont de l'Alpe (4hr 25min).

L'Alpe du Lauzet has a pretty little church and a fine display of wild flowers in spring.

WALK 38
L'Aiguillette du Lauzet Circuit

Start/finish	Le Pont de l'Alpe (1710m, UTM 32T 300338 4988118)
Distance	11.5km
Ascent/descent	1070m
Grade	Hard
Time	4hr 45min
Maximum altitude	2713m
Map	IGN 3436ET Meije Pelvoux (1:25,000) or IGN 3535OT Névache (1:25,000)
Refreshments	None
Access	From Briançon head NW on the D1091. Shortly after the village of le Lauzet, arrive at le Pont de l'Alpe. There is little else here except for an auberge. Cross the bridge and immediately afterwards there is a parking area on the right

Save this walk for a fine day: it's sure to be nothing less than a highlight of anyone's mountain walking holiday. If you want to see Bouquetin then this is as good a place as any to try your luck. The route makes a circuit of l'Aiguillette du Lauzet (2717m), taking in an unnamed peak (2713m) and the Col du Chardonnet Sud.

The views are a delight, and the climb and descent are (save for a few small sections) not too steep. A variation of the route can be undertaken using one of the best via ferratas in France (see 'Via ferrata' in the Introduction).

From the car park, walk back across the bridge in the direction of Briançon and immediately, turn left up a track signposted to l'Alpe de Lauzet. Shortly afterwards, ignore a path heading up to the left and keep on the track to the right. The track takes you to the S, under the W face of l'Aiguillette du Lauzet.

After 5-10min, where the main track bears round to the left, take a faint track to the E on your right. Be careful as this junction would be easy to miss. After a while the track becomes a path and winds its way steeply uphill. ▶

After about 1hr, cross a rocky gully to arrive at a junction of paths. Turn right and, after 100m, take a path heading N on the left by a cairn (UTM 32T 301593 4987395). This junction would be easy to miss so take care. As you get higher, the views towards the snow-capped peaks of the Écrins National Park are fantastic.

From the path you get fantastic views up the Vallon du Fontenil to the SW (Walk 36).

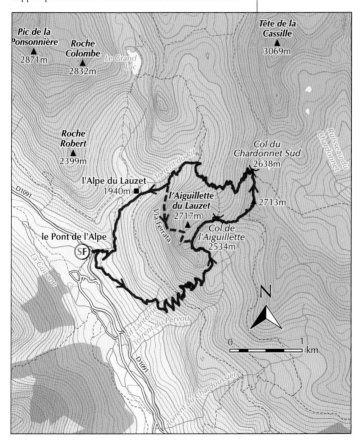

There are often Bouquetin in this area.

After 1hr 50min, arrive onto a grassy plateau and keep ahead along the path, initially to the NE. Here you enter a remote mountain bowl with few signs of human habitation. ◄

Soon the path climbs steeply, eventually heading straight towards **l'Aiguillette du Lauzet** itself. Arrive at a fork – do not take the left fork which is the path to descend from the via ferrata. Instead, take the right fork to traverse the E face of the l'Aiguillette du Lauzet. Soon the path heads across a large boulder field – there are cairns to mark the way. Shortly afterwards, arrive at the **Col de l'Aiguillette** (2534m, 2hr 25min).

At the col turn right (E) and ascend the crest of the ridge. If you thought the route was beautiful up to this point, then take a deep breath as it gets really special from here. The path becomes faint in places but just keep heading up the ridge, to the E initially, and then to the NE. Arrive at the top of an **unnamed peak** (2713m, 3hr).

Bouquetins grazing at Col de l'Aiguillette

The **views** from here are simply out of this world. To the W you look straight onto l'Aiguillette du Lauzet and to the E into the Clarée Valley.

From the peak, descend briefly N to **Col du Chardonnet Sud** (2638m). At the col, turn left and head generally W on a faint path, which is indicated by some red and white waymarks from time to time.

After 45min from the Col du Chardonnet Sud the path descends to meet the **Torrent du Rif** at a signpost. Turn left in the direction of 'le Pont de l'Alpe'. After another 10–15min, keep ahead ignoring a small path on the left which is the starting point for the via ferrata – it is not terribly well signposted.

Soon arrive at **l'Alpe du Lauzet** (1940m, 4hr 20min). Keep the buildings to your right and descend SW on a path through pastures facing onto the Écrins National Park. Eventually, the path meets a track: turn left and continue descending. Just after a waterfall turn right down a path heading back towards le Pont de l'Alpe, which can be seen below. Arrive back at your car 4hr 45min from the start.

The Chapel at l'Alpe du Lauzet

WALK 39

Lacs du Glacier d'Arsine

Start/finish	Col du Lautaret (2050m, UTM 32T 295466 4989903)
Distance	21km
Ascent/descent	670m
Grade	Very hard
Time	6hr 20min
Maximum altitude	2463m
Map	IGN 3436ET Meije Pelvoux (1:25,000)
Refreshments	Refuge de l'Alpe
Access	From Briançon, head NW on the D1091. Pass over Col du Lautaret. Then, just after the road bends around to the right, there is a parking area on the left with an information board.

The first hour of this route is all about la Meije (one of the highest peaks in the Écrins National Park) as it involves a stunning balcony path with incredible views of this imposing peak and its glaciers. Then there is a long and unusually gentle climb up a beautiful green valley within the Écrins National Park. After reaching a lovely broad col, you then climb to two high Alpine lakes set below the Glacier d'Arsine. This long walk is an amazing day out.

The entire route is on clear paths so navigation is straightforward. The altitude gain and loss are not prohibitive but the route is very long. The first 90min are more demanding than they would appear from the map because the path undulates relentlessly as it contours around the side of the mountain.

From the information board in the car park, take a path heading S (signposted 'Refuge de l'Alpe'). Shortly afterwards, at a junction, turn right (signposted 'Col d'Arsine'). The path soon heads towards the W in the direction of la Meije and its glaciers (which are with you from the get go). For the first few km, there are some very

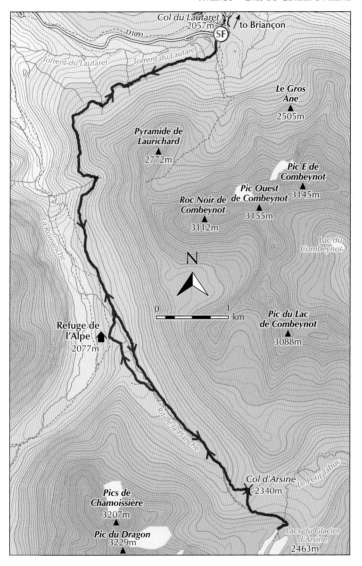

interesting information boards: non-French speakers will be disappointed, but the amazing views should be some consolation.

After 45min, the path bends to the left to head S. The exposure on the right-hand side of the path is thrilling here as there are sheer drops down into the Romanche Valley. **A fall here would be extremely serious.** Soon the path makes its way around the edges of a combe, crossing a stream in the middle of it.

There is another valley visible to the S where the source of the Romanche river is located.

Eventually, arrive at a junction of paths (1hr 40min) – keep straight ahead (signposted 'Col d'Arsine'). The path makes its way SE up a valley. ◄

After 10–15min, arrive at another junction – keep left, still SE (signposted 'Col d'Arsine'). You will see Refuge de l'Alpe below on the right.

The shark fin shaped Pic Gaspard is one of the most recognisable features of the Écrins National Park

After a long, gentle climb, the path begins to ascend in earnest as it heads up a grassy spur to the SE. Shortly afterwards, arrive at the **Col d'Arsine** (2340m, 3hr). At the col, turn right (S) to follow a path with cairns (signposted 'Lacs du Glacier d'Arsine').

Soon, the path gets very rocky and climbs reasonably steeply to arrive at the first of the **Lacs du Glacier d'Arsine** (2463m, 3hr 25min). Turn left and follow the path S to head to the second lake. To the S, the Glacier d'Arsine can be seen and behind it is the Montagne des Agneaux.

To descend from the lakes, retrace your steps. At the bottom of the slope before the col, turn right at some cairns to return to the col. From the col, retrace your steps down the grassy spur and then the valley (NW) until you reach a junction with a signpost – turn left (signposted 'Refuge de l'Alpe'). Shortly afterwards, cross a footbridge and continue on a path on the other side, heading generally NW. ▶

When the path reaches a grassy track, turn left to arrive at **Refuge de l'Alpe** (2077m) where refreshments should be available in summer.

From the refuge, head N and pick up a grassy path. After a few minutes, cross a river on a bridge and continue on one of the paths heading N. After a few minutes, the path arrives at a junction – turn left (signposted 'Villar d'Arêne). This is the path travelled on earlier (which you will now follow back to the start).

At the next junction, keep right (signposted 'Col du Lautaret') and retrace your steps all the way back to the start (6hr 20min).

As you descend, the mountain shaped like a shark's fin to the W is Pic Gaspard.

WALK 40
Plateau d'Emparis

Start/finish	Le Chazelet (1810m, UTM 32T 286379 4992464)
Distance	17.5km
Ascent/descent	1015m
Grade	Hard
Time	6hr
Maximum altitude	2460m
Map	IGN 3435ET Valloire (1:25,000) and IGN 3335ET Le Bourg d'Oisans/l'Alpe d'Huez (1:25,000)
Refreshments	Le Chazelet
Access	From Briançon head NW on the D1091. Pass over the Col du Lautaret. After the village of Villar-d'Arène, pass through the Tunnel des Ardoisières. Soon afterwards, immediately before the Tunnel du Serre du Coin, turn left onto the D33 (signposted 'le Chazelet'). After 2.5km arrive at a junction – turn left in the direction of 'le Chazelet'. After another 2.5km arrive at the village of le Chazelet. There is a parking area at the entrance to the village. If this car park is full, head back along the road for a few metres (away from le Chazelet) and turn left in the direction of a car park sign – this road brings you up over to the N side of the village where there is parking in the verges.

This walk is not technically in the Guisane Valley. Rather it is in the Romanche Valley, but let's not let semantics get in the way of what could be one of the best walks of your life. The walk involves an astoundingly beautiful traverse a stone's throw from la Meije, one of the highest mountains in the Écrins National Park, which is surrounded by glaciers. The route also passes two fabulous lakes which on a still day will have the reflection of la Meije etched into them. Make no mistake, this route should be at the top of your bucket list.

The walk is on clear paths save for a steep rocky section with cairns before Lac Noir. The two climbs on the route are steep but don't let that put you off because you can relax on the sublime traverse which breaks them up. Navigation is straightforward and there are often red and white waymarks for guidance.

There are some sheer drops along the edges of the plateau between the lakes so watch where you stray: avoid this walk in low visibility. In any case, the route is so good on a sunny day that it would be a great shame to undertake it if it was cloudy.

From the car park, follow a sign for 'GR54 Plateau d'Emparis' and walk through the village on the road. After a few minutes, the road starts to descend as it leaves the village. At a road junction, keep left (signposted 'Plateau d'Emparis') and continue to descend.

After a few minutes, arrive at a junction of tracks – keep left (signposted 'Plateau d'Emparis GR54'). After a few more minutes, cross a bridge and immediately afterwards, turn left to climb a path heading uphill to the S from the base of a chairlift. After 5–10min arrive at a junction – keep right (signposted 'Plateau d'Emparis GR54'). ▶

On the relentless climb it is tempting to stop and take photographs as la Meije feels very close. But hold fire as the views will get even better.

There are lots of interlinking paths on the climb but do not worry as they all end up in the same place. 1hr from the start, arrive at a signpost near a pair of benches – keep heading uphill (signposted 'Plateau d'Emparis GR54'). After another 20min, arrive at the start of the Plateau d'Emparis' where you will surely hear the soothing sound of cow bells from the herds that graze here in the summer months. You can now get your camera out!

Keep on the path (initially to the NW) as it traverses the plateau by contouring around the hillside. The next 3–4hr of the route are quite simply as good as it gets.

Eventually, the path arrives at a junction (2hr) – take the path on the right (W). After another 10 minutes, arrive at a junction with a signpost – keep straight ahead to the N (signposted 'Col du Souchet'). A few minutes later, arrive at **Col du Souchet** (2365m, 2hr 15min).

At the col, keep straight ahead towards the N (signposted 'Plateau d'Emparis') still on the GR54. After a few

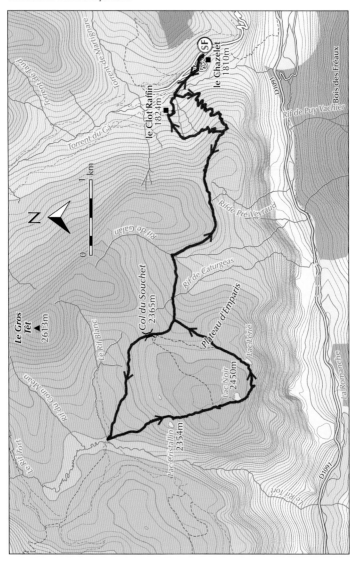

The stunning Plateau d'Emparis

minutes, the path begins to descend. When it levels off again, ignore a track on the right and keep ahead (W).

Eventually, the path descends to a signpost at a stream (3hr). From here, turn left and take a grassy path heading steeply uphill to the SE (signposted 'Lac Noir'). Where the path becomes rocky, follow the cairns. After 20–25min of steep climbing, arrive at a signpost – the path to the right takes you to **Lac Cristallin** after a few metres. But to continue to Lac Noir, take the path (at the signpost) which heads up to the S instead (cairns).

After another 10–15min of steep climbing, arrive on a grassy plateau directly facing la Meije. Keep straight ahead on the path, which passes a number of small lakes (which often dry up). After a few minutes, the path passes along the E edge of a little lake and then bears around to the SE. After a few more minutes, arrive at **Lac Noir** (2450m, 3hr 45min), a very fine place indeed for a picnic.

Take the path heading S around the W side of Lac Noir (signposted 'Lac Lérié'). At the S end of the lake, take a path heading uphill to the SE – ignore the path that heads to the left along the side of the lake. The views now get even better (if that is possible). Soon the path bends around to the E and begins to descend. ▶

If you are lucky, you may spot some Edelweiss alongside the path here but please do not pick them as they are rare.

*La Meije reflected
in Lac Lérié*

Eventually, the path heads down to **Lac Lérié** (4hr) and continues along its W side. After the lake, the path heads NE. After another 10min, the path arrives at a junction – keep right (signposted 'le Chazelet'). When this path arrives at the traverse path you walked earlier, turn right and follow the traverse to the E. The traverse was so good the first time, why not do it again!

Eventually, you will see le Chazelet again down below. When you arrive at the signpost and benches you passed earlier, turn left (signposted 'le Clot Raffin'). This path is not quite as steep as the one used earlier to ascend and eventually, it arrives at the little hamlet of **le Clot Raffin** (1824m, 5hr 40min).

From here, turn right down a grassy track – there is a wooden sign to 'le Chazelet' but it is hard to spot. The track enters a field and disappears – head SE to pick up the track again (after a few metres) and descend rather steeply to arrive at the bridge you crossed earlier. Cross the bridge and climb the track to le Chazelet. Walk through the village back to the start (6hr).

APPENDIX A
Route summary table

Walk no	Walk name	Start	Grade	Distance (km)	Time	Total ascent (m)	Maximum altitude (m)	Page
Clarée Valley								
1	Col de Dormillouse	La Draye	Hard	14	5hr 30min	1100	2445	40
2	Fort de l'Olive and Fort de Lenlon	Plampinet	Hard	17	6hr	1050	2508	47
3	Col des Thures	Névache	Hard	14.25	4hr 25min	740	2220	52
4	Lac Noir	Névache	Hard	12.5	4hr 50min	825	2400	56
5	Refuge de Bufière by the Côte Rouge	Névache	Medium	10	3hr 50min	620	2157	60
6	Pic du Lac Blanc via Lac Laramon & Lac du Serpent	Fontcouverte	Very hard/ medium	14.5/8.5	6hr 15min/3hr	1130/590	2980/2448	64
7	Col des Muandes	Laval	Hard	15.75	5hr 45min	945	2828	69
8	Tour of the Massif des Cerces	Laval	Very hard	18	6hr 45min	1050	2788	73
Montgenèvre								
9	Le Chenaillet	Montgenèvre	Hard	13	5hr 10min	895	2650	80
10	Fort du Gondran	Montgenèvre	Medium	11.5	3hr 30min	638	2459	85
11	Mont Chaberton	Montgenèvre	Very hard	17.5	6hr 40min	1295	3131	91

Walk no	Walk name	Start	Grade	Distance (km)	Time	Total ascent (m)	Maximum altitude (m)	Page
Cerveyrette Valley								
12	Alp du Pied	Cervières	Easy	3.75	1hr 45min	280	1915	98
13	Fort de la Lausette & the Peygus	Le Laus	Very hard	14.5	6hr 10min	1070	2612	101
14	Col de Bousson	Le Bourget	Easy	6.75	2hr 10min	340	2170	106
15	Lac des Cordes	Le Bourgea	Medium	10	3hr 45min	680	2601	110
Ayes Valley								
16	Lac du Plan Vallon	Le Mélézin	Easy	6.5	2hr 45min	438	2315	116
17	Col des Ayes	Plan Peyron	Medium	11	3hr 30min	612	2477	120
18	Fort de la Croix de Bretagne & la Grande Maye	Villard-St-Pancrace	Very hard	18.5	6hr	1180	2417	124
19	Lac de l'Orceyrette	Plan Peyron	Easy	8.5	3hr	355	2183	130
Durance Valley								
20	Lac Palluel and Lac Faravel	Dormillouse	Hard	14	5hr 10min	1080	2479	136
21	Lac de Fangeas	Dormillouse	Medium	7	2hr 40min	550	1990	141
22	Dormillouse High Circuit	Dormillouse	Medium	7.75	2hr 45min	580	1850	144
23	Crête de la Rortie	Les Roberts	Medium	10.25	3hr 20min	660	1763	149
24	La Grande Cabane	Deslioures	Hard	15	5hr	790	2254	153
25	La Blanche	Puy Aillaud	Very hard	12	6hr	1400	2953	158
26	Chapelle St Hippolyte	D4 near Prelles	Easy	4	1hr 30min	270	1501	162

Walk no	Walk name	Start	Grade	Distance (km)	Time	Total ascent (m)	Maximum altitude (m)	Page
27	Croix de la Salcette	Bouchier	Hard	10.5	4hr	870	2331	165
28	Cime de la Condamine	Les Combes	Very hard	14.5	6hr 40min	1150	2940	169
29	La Croix d'Aquila	Les Combes	Medium	12	4hr 10min	720	2466	175
Guisane Valley								
30	Briançon and Fort des Sallettes	Briançon	Easy	7	2hr 10min	350	1533	182
31	La Croix de Toulouse	Briançon	Medium	9.5	3hr 10min	650	1973	186
32	Circuit of le Grand Area	Bergerie Saint Joseph	Hard	15.75	6hr	800	2483	190
33	La Grande Peyrolle by the Crête de Peyrolle	Col de Granon	Medium	10.25	3hr 40min	570	2645	194
34	Grand Lac de l'Oule	Col de Granon	Easy	6.5	2hr 20min	290	2564	198
35	La Cime des Conchiers	Le Monêtier-les-Bains	Medium	7.75	3hr	485	1935	201
36	Lac de Combeynot	Les Boussardes	Hard	8.25	3hr 50min	930	2555	206
37	Les Arêtes de la Bruyère	Le Pont de l'Alpe	Hard	9.75	4hr 25min	734	2440	209
38	L'Aiguillette du Lauzet Circuit	Le Pont de l'Alpe	Hard	11.5	4hr 45min	1070	2713	214
39	Lacs du Glacier d'Arsine	Col du Lautaret	Very hard	21	6hr 20min	670	2463	218
40	Plateau d'Emparis	Le Chazelet	Hard	17.5	6hr	1015	2460	222

APPENDIX B

Hill forts

Around Briançon there are approximately 20 forts. They were constructed over the years to protect against a variety of enemies and have had a variety of occupants, including Napoleon's forces and the Italian and German armies during the Second World War. Many of the forts have been designated as world heritage sites by UNESCO. Some of the forts are permanently open but others are not. For rights of access and opening hours of many of the forts you should check with the Briançon tourist office.

A summary of the key fortifications of Briançon and their approximate dates of construction is set out below. This is far from a complete list as the remains of military buildings in the Briançonnais are too numerous to list exhaustively.

Main city fortifications

- **Fort du Château** is set on a high outcrop above the old town and was designed to repel an attack on Briançon from the NE. The current fort was built between 1835 and 1845.

- **Fort des Salettes** (see Walks 30 and 31) was envisioned by military engineer Marquis de Vauban (1633–1707), but the original structure was built after his death, between 1709 and 1712. Alterations took place between 1835 and 1855.

- **Fort des Trois Têtes** overlooks Fort du Château. Part of Vauban's vision, but built after his death between 1721 and 1734.

- **Fort du Randouillet** overlooks Fort des Trois Têtes. Part of Vauban's vision but built after his death between 1721 and 1734.

- **Communication Y** is a 200m covered passageway between Fort des Trois Têtes and Fort du Randouillet, designed to seal off the gap between the forts giving a continuous line of fortifications. It was built between 1721 and 1734.

- **Fort Dauphin** overlooks the hamlet of le Fontenil. It offered protection for the Fort des Trois Têtes and was completed towards the middle of the 18th century.

- **Fort d'Anjou** overlooks Fort du Randouillet. It was built in the 1730s.

East Fortifications

These were built to protect Briançon from attack from the Clarée or Cerveyrette Valleys.

- **Fort de l'Infernet** was built in 1875. Its high altitude (2377m) provided its artillery with a very long reach.

- **Forts du Gondran** (A to D) (see Walk 10) were built between 1876 and 1910.

- **Fort du Janus** was built between 1886 and 1903. Subterranean buildings and artillery positions were added between 1931 and 1937 as part of the Maginot Line (see below).

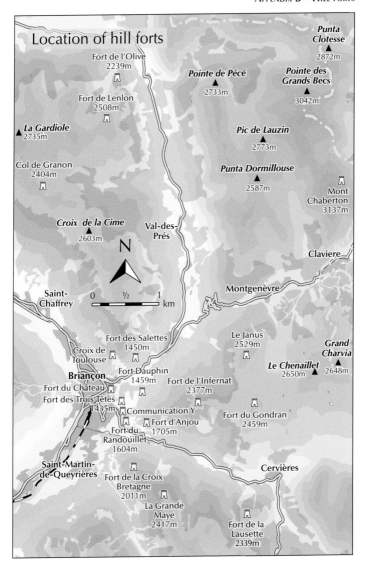

Location of hill forts

Punta Clotesse 2872m

Fort de l'Olive 2239m

Pointe de Pécé 2733m

Pointe des Grands Becs 3042m

Fort de Lenlon 2508m

La Gardiole 2735m

Pic de Lauzin 2773m

Col de Granon 2404m

Punta Dormillouse 2587m

Mont Chaberton 3137m

Croix de la Cime 2603m

Val-des-Prés

Claviere

N

Saint-Chaffrey

0 ½ 1 km

Montgenèvre

Fort des Salettes 1450m

Le Janus 2529m

Grand Charvia 2648m

Croix de Toulouse

Le Chenaillet 2650m

Briançon

Fort-Dauphin 1459m

Fort de l'Infernat 2377m

Fort du Chateau

Fort des Trois Têtes 1435m

Communication Y

Fort d'Anjou 1705m

Fort du Gondran 2459m

Fort du Randouillet 1604m

Saint-Martin-de-Queyrières

Cervières

Fort de la Croix Bretagne 2011m

La Grande Maye 2417m

Fort de la Lausette 2339m

South-east Fortifications

These were built to protect Briançon from attack from the Cerveyrette Valley

- **Fort de la Croix de Bretagne** (see Walk 18) was built between 1874 and 1879 at 2011m on an outcrop above the village of Villar-St-Pancrace.

- **La Grande Maye** (see Walk 18), built around 1885, overlooks Fort de la Croix de Bretagne.

- **Fort de la Lausette** (see Walk 13) was built around 1887–1889.

North Fortifications

These were built to protect Briançon from attack from the Clarée Valley or the Guisane Valley

- **Fort de l'Olive** (see Walk 2) was built between 1881 and 1883 to control the Col de l'Echelle and the Col des Thures.

- **Fort de Lenlon** (see Walk 2) was built between 1891 and 1893 to protect Fort de l'Olive.

- **Col du Granon** military barracks (see Walks 33 and 34) were built in the 1890s.

- **La Croix de Toulouse** barracks and gun emplacements (see Walk 31), overlooking Briançon's old town, were built between 1876 and 1914.

Forts of the Maginot Line

This defensive line of fortifications (named after the then French Minister of War, André Maginot) was built in the 1930s along the E borders of France to protect against a German or Italian invasion from the E.

- **Fort du Gondran** (E) (see Walk 10) was built from 1935–1939.

APPENDIX C
Useful contacts

Emergency services 112

Tourist information
Briançon
tel +33 (0)4 92 21 08 50
Email: info@ot-briancon.fr
www.ot-briancon.fr

Vallouise
tel +33 (0)4 92 23 36 12
www.tourisme-lavallouise.com

Névache
tel +33 (0)4 92 20 02 20
www.nevache-tourisme.fr

Montgenèvre
tel +33 (0)4 92 21 52 52
www.montgenevre.com

Le Monetier-les-Bains
tel +33 (0)4 92 24 98 98
www.serrechevalier.com
www.serre-chevalier.com

La Grave
tel +33 (0)4 76 79 90 05
www.lagrave-lameije.com

Bus services
Resalp
tel +33 (0)4 92 20 47 50)
www.autocars-resalp.com

Lignes Express Régionales
www.info-ler.fr

Train
SNCF
http://en.oui.sncf

Accommodation
Alp Base (self-catering accommodation
in the Vallouise Valley)
tel +33 (0)4 92 23 45 69
or +44 (0)871 218 0080
www.alpbase.com

Logis Hotels
www.logishotels.com

Weather
www.meteofrance.com

APPENDIX D
Bibliography and further reading

A Wild Herb Soup – The life of a French Countrywoman by Emilie Carles (1977)

Via Ferratas of the French Alps by Richard Miller (Cicerone Press, 2014) – detailed information on all the via ferratas in the French Alps including those referred to in this book

The History of Serre Chevalier and Briançon by Susan Lomas (CreateSpace, 2012) – an exceptionally thorough book, written in English, on the history of the Briançonnais

Les Fortifications des Alpes de Vauban à Maginot by Robert Bornecque (Le Dauphiné Éditions, 2012)

Sentinelles des Alpes, Citadelles et Fortifications by Yves Barde (Editions Ouest-France, 2010)

Fleurs des Montagnes by D. and R. Aichele, H. Werner and A. Schwegler (Vigot, 2007)